Train Up Your Child...
A Guide for Christian Parents

Earline Doak Kendall & Betty Doak Elder

Abingdon
Nashville

TRAIN UP YOUR CHILD . . .

Copyright © 1980 by Abingdon

All rights reserved.
No part of this book may be reproduced in any manner whatsoever without written permission of the publisher except brief quotations embodied in critical articles or reviews. For information address Abingdon, Nashville, Tennessee.

Library of Congress Cataloging in Publication Data

KENDALL, EARLINE DOAK, 1935–
  Train up your child.
  Bibliography: p. 110
  1. Christian education of children.
  I. Elder, Betty Doak, 1938–   joint author.
  II. Title.
  BV1475.2.K44   649'.7   79-21103

ISBN 0-687-42477-1

Unless otherwise indicated, scripture quotations are from *The Living Bible,* copyright © 1971 Tyndale House Publishers, Wheaton, Illinois. Used by permission.

The scripture quotation noted NEB is from The New English Bible. © the Delegates of the Oxford University Press and the Syndics of the Cambridge University Press 1961, 1970. Reprinted by permission.

MANUFACTURED BY THE PARTHENON PRESS AT
NASHVILLE, TENNESSEE, UNITED STATES OF AMERICA

For our mother,
in memory of our father
. . . and for our sons

ACKNOWLEDGMENTS

The joy and trauma of writing this book have been gratefully shared with Jay, Craig, and Mark, and with those who read an early draft and made suggestions: Don Finto, Kent McNish, Tina and Barry Boggs, Donna Roseberry, Libby Bearden, Mary Dillingham, Alma May Scarborough, and Mozelle Core, who has served as our most continuous supporter and faithful critic. Much of chapter 8 reflects the teaching of John Lane Denson. Gary Gore made format suggestions, and Pat Bryan added a professional touch with a typed first draft.

The final push to finish was made possible through the prayerful support of many and by the typing and "cheering on" provided by Mary Ellen Drushal.

EDK
BDE

CONTENTS

INTRODUCTION 9

CHAPTER ONE
  Reasons for Spiritual Training 13

CHAPTER TWO
  Where and When to Begin 21

CHAPTER THREE
  Unconditional Love 29

CHAPTER FOUR
  Positive Self-Concepts 33

CHAPTER FIVE
  Who Is in Charge Here? 45

CHAPTER SIX
  Training for Christian Living 63

CHAPTER SEVEN
  Dealing with Moral Problems 77

CHAPTER EIGHT
  *The Place of Ritual and Doctrine
  in Spiritual Training* 90

CHAPTER NINE
  Releasing Our Children 100

ANNOTATED BIBLIOGRAPHY 107

Betsy and Susan, ages four and five, were asked by their grandmother what they wanted more than anything in the whole world.

>Betsy: A hundred thousand jelly beans.
>Susan: To know what's right and do it.

INTRODUCTION

The Bible says, "Train up a child in the way he should go: and when he is old, he will not depart from it" (Prov. 22:6 KJV). This is our most basic charge as parents, our most constant concern, and our greatest challenge. Life—and God himself—could scarcely ask more of us, and we cannot afford, as parents or as human beings, to respond with less than our very best efforts.

But how do we do that?

Beginning with Mary and Joseph, Christian parents have sought the answer to that question. Undoubtedly, down through the ages, many have failed. The answers never have been easy, and in today's world, the questions are even more complicated and overwhelming. When we think we have the answers, we often find we do not; and when we are most certain we have failed, we sometimes discover, perhaps years later, that we have not. We scarcely know how to measure our progress, much less how to chart our course.

The demands on us as parents are so great and so constant that we can barely keep up with "the minimum daily requirements"; we feel no need to borrow trouble from seemingly remote issues, such as moral behavior and spiritual development. Out of necessity, we tend to focus on the most pressing need of the moment. We find ourselves going, if not from crisis to crisis, then at least from need to need. When our children are ill, our primary concern is their recovery; their social, intellectual, emotional, and spiritual development scarcely have priority. When they withdraw and refuse to make friends, we worry about their social adjustment, not their intellectual progress or spiritual well-being. At those times, what we want most is for them to act like normal children who go outdoors and play. When they fail in school, we find ourselves preoccupied with homework and report cards—not with what the pediatrician or the basketball coach, or even with what the Sunday school teacher has to say.

In these critical, demanding instances, we do not respond by keeping silent. We do not say "A fever is nothing to worry about" or "This is just an awkward stage" or "We don't want to confuse them by offering advice." We do not hesitate to take action.

Though we may see our children's spiritual well-being as our greatest long-term concern and their moral, spiritual, and religious training as their greatest long-term requirement, we still find ourselves at a loss as to what to do about these needs from day to day. We are often afraid to take moral and religious stands with our children until we are forced to do so, but if we wait until our backs are against the wall, it is often too late. We are afraid to say, "In our house, this is the way we do things," for fear that ours may not be the best way—or even a good way. We may even wait until our children are teen-agers in trouble, or until they are young adults already making decisions on their own, before we try

Introduction

to help, and then we may issue admonitions, warnings, and platitudes.

What has become of our confidence in what we have to offer our children? Do we place so little stock in the guidance we have to give, and as parents, do we possess so little hope, that we have nothing of substance to contribute?

We realize that fulfilling the needs of our children involves more than providing physical care, educational opportunity, material abundance, and appropriate social contact. Just as we are unwilling to leave their health, social adjustment, intellectual progress, and emotional maturation to chance, we do not *want* to leave their moral and spiritual growth to chance either. We believe we owe them guidance as well as acceptance, direction as well as openness, definitive standards rather than indulgence, and training rather than a laissez-faire coexistence. Acting out of the courage of our convictions, we *want* to take a stand about spiritual and moral values. We are not content to leave the teaching of moral behavior to the school or the teaching of religion to the church.

But the question is: How do we, the parents, go about taking an active part in the moral and spiritual training of our children?

This book attempts to guide and encourage parents in their quest for answers to this question and others related to it. Though some advice of a how-to nature is included, this book is not intended to get you through the day or the week, as much as it is designed to help you through the nights of self-doubt and the years of self-examination that inevitably accompany parenthood.

As parents, we are all guilty of countless oversights, lapses, and transgressions that, given the opportunity, we would change or undo. We are often found lacking—in courage, faith, humility, humor, love, wisdom, and upon occasion, even simple good sense. In many ways, we grow up with our children; our pilgrimage becomes theirs and theirs ours. We learn from them as much as we teach. In the end, if we had it to do over again, we would seek more answers at the outset. We would be older and wiser, more patient and more certain. And more successful. But, if courage is grace under pressure, then surely grace, at least in part, is the ability to forgive oneself lost opportunities. Much as parents are called upon to accept children for who they are, our children are called upon to accept us, not only for who we are, but for where they happen to find us when they come into our lives.

So, unprepared and ill-equipped as all parents are, we must do our best. This book is an attempt to examine how parents can do their best for their children.

CHAPTER ONE

Reasons for Spiritual Training

Spiritual training is a daily acting out of commitment and recommitment of ourselves to God and to our children, that they may grow in "wisdom and stature and favor with God and man."

Why should I offer spiritual training and religious teaching to my children?

There are several answers to that question. One is, for their sake; another, for our own.

As Christian parents, we can scarcely do otherwise. Our commitment to God includes the commitment of our children. The releasing of our children to God becomes our greatest gift—a "sacrifice" in much the same way that Abraham brought Isaac to the altar.

The commitment of our children to God is not only our greatest gift to God—a supreme act of love—but our greatest gift to our children. When we can offer nothing else dependable and constant, what greater gift than faith? Only God promises to be the same today, tomorrow, and forever.

This is the Good News—and the best news we have to pass along to our children is that the covenant relationship we rely upon with God has become the stabilizing center of our life and can become the stabilizing center of theirs. Would we deny them this Good News?

But don't they have to find this out for themselves?

Yes, and they will. They won't let us do the hard part for them. Most of us turn to God only when there is nowhere else to turn. We look in every direction, and finally, after all else fails, we come back to God. Though we would spare our children such a search, we probably can't—not if they are thoughtful, searching, spiritually hungry people. They will not be content to "piggyback" on our faith, or on that of anyone else. What we have to offer them is not a ready-made faith and set of beliefs but an invitation for them to share our search and for us to share theirs.

Is it their nature to need religion, or do we impose this need on them?

Even nonreligious parents find their children asking questions about religion—and wanting their questions heard and respected and responded to thoughtfully and lovingly. Even when they are very young, children seek answers about God, death, heaven, the devil, and the mysteries these topics suggest. When their questions are given no encouragement, or when they become distrustful of the answers, or of those who give them, they may search elsewhere.

Adolescence and early adulthood is often a time of challenging one's religious heritage and arriving at some conclusions—perhaps new approaches of one's own. Young people who have no family religion to push off from will seek to fill this void, and at this

Reasons for Spiritual Training

point in their lives, they may be particularly vulnerable to easy answers. Having no role models at home for a religious life or quest, they follow those they find elsewhere—and their parents may feel that these are strange and undesirable.

In recent years, the popularity of Eastern cults and esoteric sects speaks of the spiritual hunger of American young people, whether we, as parents, raise religious issues with them or not. A revived interest in fairy tales, astrology, magic, ESP, and the impact on our culture of stories such as *Star Wars* and those about the Hobbit, reflect a spiritual longing for the mystical in people of all ages.

The search for personal growth and spiritual wholeness has been called by many names, including "self-actualization," by Maslow and "cosmic understanding," by Kohlberg. The spiritual dimension of human development has engaged philosophical and theological minds down through the ages and, in recent times, has become the concern of educators and psychologists as well. Spiritual longing and searching is recognized not only as an integral part of a meaningful adult life, but as an integral part of childhood as well.

But can I give my children support without passing along my own uncertainties?

Our children can accept us and our uncertainties more easily than they can cast about alone for a way to reach spiritual satisfaction. The way they find may offer mystery and even mysticism, but still may not include Christian grace and love. Although, to some extent, each of us must make the journey alone, to let our children stumble about without our support leaves them vulnerable to counterfeits that may lead them, not to God and a fulfilling relationship in his service, but into shallow, and even dangerous, beliefs that will never satisfy.

How will my own life be enriched if I give spiritual training to my children?

Spiritual training means sharing in and enriching one another's lives. When parents do that for their children, their children in turn do that for them. Although great discipline is involved, spiritual training is not something that is forced upon children by their parents. It is a daily living-out of commitment to God and to one another; it is, in essence, saying to our children, "Your growth and well-being are my greatest concern, and sharing in your growth enriches my life and makes me a better person."

Does this mean that children have as much to offer us as we have to offer them?

No. They undoubtedly have more to offer, in some ways. But what we have to offer is not comparable to their offering.

What is this difference between parents and children?

Because we are bigger, older, and more experienced, we have responsibilities they don't have. These responsibilities include meeting the legal, financial, cultural, physical, and religious needs of our children. In other words, as parents, we are in charge and are held accountable.

Does this mean we are responsible for what they become?

Not entirely, but we are responsible for having brought them into the world. Somehow, whether

Reasons for Spiritual Training

consciously or unconsciously, we *chose* to have these children, and they had no choice whatsoever in their own births.

Yes, but isn't a home supposed to be democratic, with everybody having a voice in the decisions?

A home is not a democracy, certainly, although all members of the family take their turns at making decisions of which they are capable. This, however, does not mean that we abdicate our responsibility for the home to our children. Children are a minority in the home, if not in numbers, at least legally and financially. As a nation recently grown conscientious about our treatment of such minorities as blacks, women, the handicapped, and the elderly, we tend to bend over backward to balance past inequities, so that now these groups may be receiving opportunities disproportionate to their numbers. In some instances, we have even begun to discriminate against the majority. Some parallel to these national trends can be seen in homes where parents are now going to extremes to give children their rights—long overdue for children, as well as for minorities—but the result, in middle-income homes particularly, can be to abdicate our responsibility to the point that sometimes it is no longer clear who is in charge and where accountability properly rests.

How can I know if I am prepared to offer spiritual training to my children?

Look at it this way—are you prepared to feed and support them? The answer is probably "only moderately so," or that you hope to do so. No one knows, until they have done the feeding and supporting, all that is involved in the 2:00 A.M. feedings, the breakfasts on the run chasing the school bus, the suppers *every* night, year in and year out, or the struggles to earn enough to pay the pediatrician, the milkman, the piano teacher, and the orthodonist. And yet, when we decide to have children, we decide to take on that care and feeding. And that care and feeding involve spiritual care and feeding, as much as any other kind of nurturing and protection.

What if the constancy of providing for my children gets on my nerves?

Welcome to the crowd! All children get on their parents' nerves. This does not mean you are a bad parent; it means that you are like all the rest of us—you are human! Jesus himself must have gotten on the nerves of Mary and Joseph. At least, we know he disappeared without telling them where he was going and didn't show up for supper. Indeed, he was about his Father's business, but his parents felt and reacted like all parents everywhere—they were worried and irritated—and nerve-wracked.

What if I don't like my children?

None of us likes our children all the time. Sometimes we find them decidedly unappealing and unlovable. Most of us love our children most of the time and find them the most interesting, fascinating creatures in the world. Even those of us who do not consider ourselves particularly fond of children in general find ourselves thrilled by our own children, as we watch them learn and grow. Sometimes, however, something goes wrong, and mothers or fathers find themselves incapable of liking and perhaps loving their children, or one of their children. This is a most serious problem, and the consequences can be tragic and heartbreaking. If parents are unable to accept and love their children, they need to come to grips with the qualities they consider unacceptable and unlovable in their children and in themselves. Nothing can be done for them or their children unless they can overcome their guilt sufficiently to acknowledge their feelings, certainly to themselves, but also to God. Then they can seek help in dealing with these feelings from the best Christian counselors available and through prayer, in the belief that God will grant them grace, forgiveness, and a change of heart—and he will!

What if I just don't enjoy being with my children?

Examine the possibility that you are with them too constantly. You and they may need a break from one another. If, after having time alone, time with stimulating adults, and time with God, you still do not enjoy your children, check to see if others do.

You may need to change their behavior (by changing yours) to help them become people others like to be with. Are they considerate, joyful, and interesting? If not, help them to develop these characteristics, so that you and others will take pleasure in their company.

What if I don't have time for spiritual training of my children?

Take the time. For God's sake, for your children's sake, and for your own sake, take the time!

But I really don't have the time or the strength or the wisdom to do this alone.

Don't do it alone. Get help. Seek God's help. Just as children cannot grow up in a vacuum, parents cannot raise them in a vacuum. All parents need support and understanding. And parenting. God can parent us as we parent our children. "He is like a father to us, tender and sympathetic" (Ps. 103:13).

CHAPTER TWO

Where and When to Begin

Christianity is a faith of renewals and new beginnings, for which it is never too late or too early.

How does spiritual training differ from moral teaching about right and wrong?

The accumulation of daily interaction between parents and children through shared experiences cannot be called *teaching,* as much as it may be termed *training.* Training of any kind, whether it be praying at bedtime, hitting a baseball, taking out the garbage, or toilet training, is not something we say or even anything we do to our children, but it is something that is built on, day by day.

I think I know how to take pretty good care of my children, but I don't even know where to start doing something as complicated as "spiritual training."

Begin by asking yourself what you want for your children and what kind of people you want them to become.

When asked these questions, most parents respond, "I don't care whether they turn out to be doctors or lawyers or rich or famous, as long as they grow up to be decent, moral people and pretty good human beings." Often they add, "I just want them to be happy."

And yet, what most parents really want is considerably more than that. Not doctors or lawyers, perhaps, or wealth or fame, but more than simple decency, nonetheless. What many of us parents really want—and may be afraid to say—is that our children have a sense of duty to meaningful work, a sense of responsibility to meaningful relationships, and a sense of "connectedness" with the world at large. Along with duty, responsibility, and connectedness, we want them to know joy, pleasure, peace of mind, love, friendship, success, happiness, adventure, excitement, fulfillment, and so on and so on. At the same time, we want them to exhibit strength of character, sound judgment, moral fiber, integrity, honesty, and so on and so on.

In other words, we want our children to have everything good and honorable, sweet and rewarding, that life has to offer. And we want them to be perfect.

No small order!

To express this in another way: We want them to have all the good things in life that we have had—and all that we have missed. And while they are about it, we want them to be better people than we ourselves are.

Are you saying I must begin by looking at myself?

Yes.

How do I do that?

Nothing puts us back in touch with the traditions of our childhood and what we ourselves were taught quite as much as having children of our own to teach.

Where and When to Begin

What most of us know about moral and religious training is what we have experienced personally. Some fortunate few of us might respond by saying, "Yes, and that's exactly what I want to give to my children." Far more of us would respond that there are some aspects of our own heritage we want to pass on and some aspects we would like to eliminate, lest they continue to frustrate, embarrass, limit, and perhaps damage, subsequent generations.

Thus, what we pass along to our children becomes a selective process. In order to sort out these aspects, we must dig deep within our own conscience, our own consciousness, and our past, to define for our children, and thus to redefine for ourselves, what devotion to the higher and more honorable values of life means to us. To do this in good faith, and with a true sense of personal awareness, is to realign ourselves with the best that our heritage has given us, that we might then pass the best of ourselves along to our children.

What about couples who don't share the same religious heritage or even the same beliefs and practices?

Not only is the selective process a trying and soul-searching task for those of us of mixed mind about our own upbringing, but it is an even more excruciating task for two people, especially if they are of different backgrounds or points of view. No two people ever have exactly the same heritage or values, although they may have very similar ones. Therefore, to work together, they have to interweave the best from each, to form the fiber of a new relationship. This is a formidable endeavor, particularly when that new relationship is to become the basis of a heritage to be passed along to children. Although it is seldom undertaken consciously, surely it is the most important issue that couples who plan to have children must face.

Religious compatibility sometimes plays a central part in the decision of couples to marry, but for many couples, the first discussion of religion occurs when they are planning the wedding ceremony. Then their joy and excitement well may be jarred by unexpected, and seemingly sudden, conflict. With the engagement announcement, the chosen one is apt to take on an extended identity. Instead of being seen only as an individual, the much-loved future spouse, in an "overnight" transition, becomes someone with family and traditions—and quite possibly, Religion. It may even seem to be a strange religion or a silly religion or too much religion or not enough religion. These "new" dimensions frequently are indications of differences far more complex and far-reaching than those of the wedding event itself.

Regrettably, when religious issues are encountered only in conjunction with public and emotional occasions, people particularly do not want to admit differences or deal with conflict. Consequently, there may be a temptation to de-emphasize differences, homogenize preferences, and go along with what is happening.

Indeed, religious issues may not come up again for some time, perhaps not until a child is born or a family crisis occurs—perhaps a death or some other landmark occasion usually accompanied by a religious observance. Intermittent postponement from one such event to the next can become habitual, until it extends over a lifetime. Many couples never learn to share their religious feelings satisfactorily, much less reach any understanding or resolution, because they shelve religious contemplation and discussion as much as possible. And yet, when ceremonial occasions or family crises occur, they may be propelled into taking a position, be it an active religious response of their own, compliance with the religious expectations of others, or a stand against religious expression altogether.

Isn't it better for religious issues to be raised at the time of a wedding or some other public ceremony, than for them never to come up at all?

Yes. Without these occasions to prod us, some of us would never get in touch with our religious selves or have the opportunity to encounter each other in a religious context.

However, when our religious experience and expression are confined to the special occasions of weddings, baptisms and confirmations, funerals, Christmas and Easter, or even to Sunday mornings, we permit ourselves only limited opportunity to explore our own spiritual needs and responses, and we limit our access to a deep relationship with God. Thus when, for occasional and ceremonial use, we adopt the beliefs and practices laid down by someone else—parents, spouse, friends, the community, or even the church—we deny ourselves, our children, and our relationship with God. When we "piggyback" on someone else's faith, guilt results, with resentment close behind, and in our own mind, traditions become dogma, culture becomes sacrosanct, ritual becomes rigid, and the unfamiliar becomes threatening.

Lest these patterns develop, we need to stay attuned to our own spiritual needs and to remain sensitive to those of our mate. We need to examine and reexamine, separately and together, our individual family traditions, training, and expectations, to distinguish the aspects that nurture us from those that impede us. We also need to consider personal religious priorities, as they are conditioned by other, more present, aspects of our life.

But what if I am already well along with my life, not just with my marriage, but with my parenting? How can I go back and start over?

Of course, none of us can go back and start over. We must search out answers at whatever point in our personal spiritual growth, and in the spiritual development of our marriage and our parenting, that we realize the need. Those who establish mutual religious concerns and practices early in their life together will be all the more richly rewarded and will find themselves more surefooted in guiding their children toward a rich religious life. Those who stumble upon religious awareness and needs later in life may share the discovery with their children in a less rooted, but more immediate and vital sense. Those single parents who find themselves raising children alone are spared the collaborative effort required to merge two sets of backgrounds, beliefs, and priorities, but are left to struggle alone, without the support and sharing that a mate can offer.

How can I find support for the spiritual guidance I try to give my children?

Whether religious needs are encountered early in a relationship, later during the married years, or as a single parent, membership in a supportive,

Where and When to Begin

caring religious community can aid our search and strengthen our faith. Parents, young or experienced, married or single, cannot raise their children by themselves; religious family life needs the supporting context of religious community life. Families need the opportunities to reinforce and sustain one another that are offered by such a framework. Some will find these opportunities within the church of their upbringing; others will need to pursue a new church identity.

Are you saying I can't offer spiritual training for my children except by raising them within the church?

Spiritual training, yes. Christian training, no. By definition, Christian training includes presenting children with a relationship and an identity within the institutional church. What that relationship is, and our definition of ourselves as church people, can vary widely, depending upon our individual preferences and needs, but we are strengthened by the knowledge that we belong to a corporate body of believers, worshiping the same God and sharing the same faith. There is strength and support in this identification, and a sense of belonging, particularly as expressed by corporate worship services.

Additional support may come also from sharing in such church activities as fellowship groups and service organizations, but the church activity that nurtures and pleases one person well may irritate and frustrate another. Opportunities for Christian fellowship and service can be found in many other places, but only the church can offer the renewal that comes with corporate Christian worship.

Children, along with their parents, feel supported

by identification with the church. Just as they need and want to be able to say about their environment at home, "This is the way we do things at *our* house," they also need and want the opportunity to say, "This is the way *our* church does things."

CHAPTER THREE
Unconditional Love

Love is our greatest gift to our children, as it is God's greatest gift to us. Our love is their introduction to his love—and to a life of blessing.

How can I give my children support?

By accepting God's unconditional love and by passing this on to our children, we give them support. We help them know God's love for them by loving them ourselves, and by showing our love in ways they can believe.

Ross Campbell, in his book *How to Really Love Your Child,* states that in his practice of child psychiatry he rarely has known parents who did not really love their children, but he frequently has known children who did not believe their parents loved them.

How can I show my children that I love them?

According to Campbell, three things convince children that their parents love them: eye contact, physical contact, and focused attention.

At what age does this contact and attention begin?

At birth. Research has begun to substantiate what mothers have long believed—that even newborn babies respond to physical contact, and that they demonstrate much more social behavior than was believed in the past.

Parents in such numbers are seeking the benefits of physical contact soon after birth that hospital practices are changing. Parents are demanding to be allowed to hold and cuddle their new babies during the first few hours following birth, so that an immediate and special bond may develop between them and the infant.

When physical contact has been established during the first days of life, focused attention is usually easier for parents. Tuning into the rhythm of their infant, a rhythm belonging to that baby alone, is important during those first days. After all, their child has just gone through the most traumatic change he or she will ever experience—being born. The baby and the parents need time to interact, time to get acquainted, time to respond, time to initiate contact with one another, and time for the parents to learn the baby's needs and how to respond to them. Love does not happen automatically—a relationship needs to be established. As the parents meet the infant's needs, a relationship will begin. When a young infant's needs are met promptly, trust is developed between the child and the parents.

As children learn to trust their parents, they will learn to be trusting people. Children who sense their parents' care, love, and concern, will readily accept God's care, love, and concern. In this way, parents introduce their children to God's love and, in return, are brought closer to God themselves. Children who are denied parental love and care have difficulty believing and accepting God's love. The parent acts as a stand-in for God during the early years.

Unconditional Love

As my children grow and begin to give negative responses, how can I continue to show them love?

At whatever age our children whine, have temper tantrums, refuse to be cooperative, reject our suggestions, or behave in a generally disagreeable or even obnoxious way, maintaining positive focused attention, let alone eye and physical contact, is almost impossible. And yet, these are apt to be the times when they need it most.

The two-year-old who screams no! at everything we say and runs in the opposite direction still needs to be loved. The ten-year-old who is interested only in sports, but in nothing we have to say, still needs our attention. The sixteen-year-old who is bored by family dinners and vacation trips still needs to be needed, and enjoyed, and included in family activities that are not boring, as well as some that are.

Children who have received these manifestations of love—focused attention, eye contact, physical contact—throughout their childhood, grow up accepting that this kind of interaction is the way people get along with one another. They in turn treat others, including their parents, this way.

What if my family has never been very close or demonstrative?

In families where contact has been minimal or strained, it takes real courage to change the pattern, but it can be changed—even in adults. Parents who rarely touched their children during their growing years can respond to, and even initiate, warm physical contact with their now-grown children. Children who missed this contact during their early years can still, as adults or as teen-agers, benefit from a warm relationship with their parents. Throughout life, new patterns of interaction are still possible and can be initiated by children or by parents.

What if my children dislike physical contact?

At any age, some people may have very different needs for physical closeness and touching than do other members of their families. Such differences often cause problems in sexual compatibility between husbands and wives. They can also cause tension or distance between parents and children.

Joyful physical contact from an adult whom the child cares about can help a reluctant child to accept touching. When Craig was two, his parents honored his lack of desire for hugging, kissing, and rocking. An exuberant cousin, however, who kept him for several months while his mother worked, "loved on" him in spite of his disinclination, and he became more responsive. Her persistence in giving him attention broke a barrier, and he was the beneficiary.

Children cannot be expected to grasp and express all their own needs. In fact, they are likely to act against their own self-interest at times, refusing the very attention and affection they need. Regardless of how self-absorbed or rejecting they may be, as they grow older, they are apt to be responsive to *our* need for *their* attention and affection. We must take the risk of asking for these indications of love from them—even when they are unwilling to accept them from us. A two-year-old may say no when asked for a hug, but when approached as a friend, a twelve- or fifteen-year-old is likely to respond with a ready ear and a willing embrace, if we ask for this attention because *we ourselves* need it.

CHAPTER FOUR

Positive Self-Concepts

As parents, we cannot love and train our children unless we first believe ourselves capable of offering love and training. Our children, in turn, will not respond to our efforts unless they believe themselves lovable and worthy of training.

How can I teach my children that they are special, worthy, and acceptable?

Among the most awesome considerations of parenthood are: (1) children will see themselves much the way their parents see them; and (2) the way they see themselves will greatly determine what kind of people they grow up to be. Parents are able to wield control and influence over their children in many ways, but none is more frightening than this self-fulfilling prophecy.

Parents who receive—and perceive—their children as special gifts from God will communicate to them the feeling that God has made them unique beings and has sent them as gifts to their parents. Parents who prayed to have children and desired the birth of each one are well on their way to committing their children to God and to committing themselves to their training to serve God's purposes. When parents accept them in this way, children sense peace, love, and caring. They come to regard themselves as acceptable human beings and as blessings to their parents.

Not all children arrive in the world with this kind of welcome; some are received as burdens, interruptions, mistakes, and holy terrors. These children are not apt to see themselves as special gifts from God, or as unique and acceptable human beings, because their parents do not see them in that way.

The mother who enrolled her young son Dennis in kindergarten with the introduction, "Mrs. Kendall, this is Dennis—Dennis the Menace," well may have been instilling in her son a self-concept as a problem and troublemaker that will follow him through life. Even then he could scarcely walk across a room without the pictures falling off the wall and the chairs turning over! He did not seem to plan destruction—it followed him—and often he seemed surprised at the havoc he wrought.

The graduate students who nicknamed their beautiful first-born—and unplanned—son The Warden probably were influencing the way that child would come to see himself.

How can I protect the positive self-concept of my children?

A child's self-concept, as well as spiritual nature and moral character, is not programmed by a single incident or even by several single incidents. It is built, instance by instance, day after day. A single isolated experience rarely makes or breaks a child; however, the accumulation of many experiences, many acts of training, many instances of shaping the

Positive Self-Concepts

direction of the child's thoughts and behavior, *does* make a difference.

Is there no way to accelerate spiritual growth so that it doesn't take so long?

Probably not. It takes a lifetime. The accumulation of daily experiences provides opportunity for growth.

The interaction during childhood between parents and children cannot be hurried because it trains children through daily, shared experiences. Training of any kind, whether it be learning to knit, kick a football, recite the Lord's prayer, or wash the dishes, is built little by little.

Children learn to talk by being with people who talk to one another and to them. First they learn syllables and discover these have meaning; then gradually, they learn words and put them together to form sentences. Children learn arithmetic concepts by building on their awareness of likes and differences, more and less, enough and too much, and by noticing that their playmates have more cookies than they have. Gradually, they also learn numbers, counting, addition, algebraic equations, and perhaps calculus.

We expect gradual growth in language and mathematics. Many early language and math experiences seem unrelated to later skills or concepts, and many of them must be taught over and over. Children who are learning to talk or to count, delight in repetition as mastery is attained.

In spiritual training also, then, we must be prepared for gradual growth, for the provision of introductory experiences that seem unrelated to remote future achievements, and for repetition and repetition and repetition, even when children show no interest in religion, in God, in us, or in what we believe. As Paul pointed out, we all need to be nurtured on spiritual milk before we are fed spiritual meat.

This sounds like a slow and time-consuming process. How can I avoid becoming discouraged?

This deliberate process causes us to feel we are taking one step forward and two back, at times, and the truth is—we are. Neither children nor parents accomplish growing "in the nurture and admonition of the Lord" (Eph. 6:4 KJV) overnight, and everyone inevitably becomes discouraged. All children occasionally are disrespectful, disobedient, uncaring, and uncooperative. They also fight with their brothers and sisters, forget to come home on time, spill their milk, lose their belongings, waste their allowance, and find some several hundred other ways to irritate and annoy us. As parents, we become impatient, disheartened, and distressed. Many of these feelings are fleeting and, given a few days or a few weeks, simply "come out in the wash." Sometimes, however, during trying periods, the stress may become so great that debilitating self-doubt is the result. Parents need additional support during these times, and perhaps even professional counseling. Certainly, when their self-concepts are on trial, parents should not suffer through their anxieties and guilt alone, and a strong and attentive Christian community can be a source of reassurance and affirmation, as well as an invaluable "reality check."

How can I teach my children my values and still expect them to think for themselves?

Parents need to realize and remember, particu-

Positive Self-Concepts

larly during difficult times, what sturdy and singular creatures these children of ours are—and they are, from the very outset. *We do not make them who they are.* Mold them, yes, but they arrive in this world as individuals. We can shape their environment, guide and influence their development, guard and protect their well-being, make life easier or harder, but they are their own people, nevertheless, and as such, they themselves are capable of exerting powerful influence.

Even during the early days and weeks of life, babies will exert their own unique authority in shaping the environment of their new homes and the behavior of their new parents. Each baby has distinctive patterns of response, behavior, and ways of engaging others. These characteristics are undoubtedly influenced by the genetic makeup of the parents, diet of the mother, prenatal care, circumstances surrounding the birth, birth order, emotional climate of the home, and a host of other factors. However, whether we are able to identify the source of the characteristics or not, each baby is born with a way of behaving and responding to the world that belongs only to that baby.

This is one reason a new baby is so special—each one is different and, consequently, always surprising. Even parents who expect to find their children interesting only after they can talk or play ball or respond like "a real person" often find themselves fascinated from the outset.

Children, even babies, sound very sturdy and powerful. Do they influence us more than we do them?

Babies who are only a few hours old can affect the responses of those around them perhaps as much as they themselves can be affected. The mother of a two-day-old baby acknowledged a report on her infant's good health and normal reactions, by asking if the baby had cried while being examined. When she heard that he had cried throughout the examination—so much so, in fact, as to interfere with the testing—she looked relieved and said, "I thought he didn't like my voice. He cried every time the nurse brought him to me." This two-day-old baby had caused his mother to doubt that she was a good mother and, further, had convinced her that he did not like her.

How can we stand up to our children and to the challenges of parenting?

Parents need particularly sturdy self-concepts. While it usually takes longer than two days, most parents can count on running into self-doubt somewhere along the way. Even those who are confident and successful in other aspects of their life are apt to be insecure about their ability to parent. How well we were parented ourselves greatly influences our self-concepts and attitudes. The style of parenting we choose is directly, if unconsciously, modeled after that of our own parents. Particularly during times of stress, the behaviors we rely on or fall back on are those that were used with us.

But what if I didn't have good parenting myself?

Many abusing parents were abused children; they were not taught that they were special gifts from God or even that they were acceptable human beings. The most consistent characteristic in the abused-child syndrome is that the abusing parent was abused as a child. (Other characteristics of the parent—sex,

Positive Self-Concepts

income, I.Q., religion, educational level, race, age—are not predictive of child abuse.) And because a childhood of abuse is a frequent characteristic, it should be viewed as a warning to those parents with this type history, so that they may try to protect their children and break the cycle. Unfortunately, the cycle usually continues; children who are abused do not feel good about themselves and assume that they deserve the abuse; this feeling of low self-esteem may carry over into adulthood, and their offspring will not receive the kind of welcome and care that says, "You are a blessing."

Does this mean that if our parents abused us, we are destined to be abusive parents?

By God's grace, we do not have to live our entire lives in bondage to negative attitudes held by our parents or to experiences we have encountered. As children, we all suffered injustice, misunderstanding, and unkindness, in varying degrees, at the hands of adults. In some ways, we all are scarred and damaged.

What if I am not good enough to teach my children spiritual values?

When we dedicate our children to God, we *re*dedicate ourselves. None of us is whole or wise enough, strong or loving enough, to raise our children alone. We are called, not only to give our children up to the Lord, but to give ourselves also. Just as our children's feelings about themselves are influenced by the way we feel about them, our feelings about them are influenced by the way we feel about ourselves. Alone, none of us feels good enough. By God's grace, we *become* good enough.

Train Up Your Child

Then how we feel about ourselves makes a big difference in how we feel about our children?

Yes. Both adults and children function more satisfactorily when they feel good about themselves. A positive self-concept frees individuals to be the most they are able to be and to become the most they are able to become.

But aren't children different from adults in the way they see themselves and the world?

The ways in which children are like us, and the ways in which they are not, are difficult for us to understand; yet an understanding of these similarities and differences is basic to all aspects of relationship with children and, consequently, to all aspects of family life, if family life is to be rewarding and fulfilling. Psychologist Jean Piaget has determined that children think differently from adults; they see the world from a different perspective. We can better foster children's physical development if we perceive the level of their motor skills; we can better stimulate their intellectual development if we comprehend the level of their vocabulary and their reasoning ability; we can better encourage their social development or reinforce their emotional growth if we understand their fears and realize their level of experience. And we can better nurture their spiritual growth if we understand how they see the world, what they need, and what we have to offer.

In a family's spiritual life, adults and children have their own gifts to contribute. We tend to think that we must bring children to our level of understanding, rather than letting them bring us to

Positive Self-Concepts

their own steadfast, innocent, cloudless vision of the world. For a little while, before their growing-up takes over, theirs is a new and perfect wisdom. They have so recently come from the Father that they experience a special bond with him and a special understanding of him.

Jesus said, "Beware that you don't look down upon a single one of these little children. For I tell you that in heaven their angels have constant access to my Father" (Matt. 18:10).

Therein lies many a mystery.

Then we should become more like our children?

Jesus also said that unless you "become as little children, you will never get into the Kingdom of Heaven" (Matt. 18:3). We must not fail to offer our children understanding, for their sake, but our own personal loss would be greater for our own failure. There is so much that we must teach our children, and so many ways in which we must guide them, that we fail to see what they can teach us.

Failure to accept children has a longstanding history. There is a story in the Bible about how they were unappreciated and thus, dismissed. "Little children were brought for Jesus to lay his hands on them and pray. But his disciples scolded those who brought them . . . But Jesus said, 'Let the little children come to me, and don't prevent them' " (Matt. 19:13, 14). Jesus' own friends—those who seemed to know him best—had such limited understanding of his teaching and of his love for little children that they tried to shield him from being bothered by them.

Even today, many who seem to know him best are sending little children away. What Christian parents want most for their children is to bring them to be

Train Up Your Child

touched by Jesus. Some of the best efforts of parents, as well as of churches, to bring little children to Jesus have the opposite effect. The reason still seems to be a lack of understanding of what Jesus was teaching.

Jesus said his kingdom belongs to little children and that only those who come to God as little children will find it. The route is not easy for many of us to find, but little children already know the way. Few of us are willing to let our children lead us. We are so sure that we must show them the way that we get in their way. In our groping for the Father, we often overlook the very attributes that offer us constant access to him.

What are these attributes? In other words, what are children like?

Jesus says we are to be as trusting as little children (Luke 10:21, 18:17). Little children who have been dealt with in a loving, predictable way have a high level of trust, and trust is one of the attributes that brings us close to God.

A second basic characteristic of children is helplessness; the human infant is the most helpless, for the longest period of time, of all new creatures. A child continues complete dependence upon those who are older and more experienced, long after leaving babyhood. The young child must look beyond self for all kinds of help. This dependence on someone else was Jesus' message to his disciples when he told them to turn to God and to become as little children.

Another universal trait of children is their almost constant hunger. Soon after they are fed, they begin asking for more.

In addition to the characteristics of trust, dependence, and hunger, is the desire to grow. This need to

Positive Self-Concepts

grow physically and to develop intellectually is a need of all children. "When I grow up" is a favorite game. "Let me do it myself," dressing-up in adult clothes, imitating parents' gestures and mannerisms, trying on adult roles in pretend games, are all indications that children want to grow up and be like their parents. Children are eager for new skills and new opportunities. They reject help even before they have grown beyond the need for a particular kind of assistance.

Children are also busy. An athlete in top form cannot keep up with a healthy two-year-old, if an effort is made to match every physical maneuver the child tries. Most mothers have frequently experienced the same frustration! Children will attempt anything—there is so much to see, touch, taste, try. They become lost in the wonder of a reflection in a puddle; the texture of the grass requires investigation; the crack in the ceiling holds mystery and intrigue. A child's play is serious work. It is so serious that it requires early rising, concentration, and repeated effort. Though adults may become bored, tired, discouraged, or afraid, children about their investigations rarely feel that it is too early, too late, too cold, too hot, too much trouble, or too expensive to try a new experience. Jesus, at the age of twelve, surprised his parents by being about his Father's business. They may have believed he was "just playing," but often when children are playing, important growth is taking place. Play is a child's work.

Another characteristic of children is forgetfulness. The necessity of repetition in dealing with children often irritates parents, but the same forgetfulness that loses lunch money, jackets, and books is also

43

quick to forget and forgive slights and injustices.

Children have the ability to live in the "now." Young children confuse the concepts of today, yesterday, and tomorrow; "today" is the only reality they have. The ability to live in the present enhances many of the other traits of children. Living in the moment, they are better able to trust, can risk being dependent, will want to eat when hungry, will grow naturally, and will be busy playing. Living in the now, it is easy to forget, because there is so much immediate living to be done.

These are some of the things little children are made of. As parents, we find our lives enriched by these characteristics, from which we can learn many lessons.

CHAPTER FIVE

Who Is in Charge Here?

In order to love and train our children, we must exercise our God-given authority. Whether, as parents, we are authoritarian, authoritative, or permissive, influences our dealing with the issues of right versus privilege, need versus demand, choice versus coercion, and discipline versus punishment.

Why is authority such an important issue between parents and children?

From the time children are born, they and their parents are in a constant struggle over who is in charge. They check to see if we are watching our business. They try us even when they want us to win. They exercise their lungs, options, and prerogatives, hoping that we will care enough to exercise ours. The homes where parents and children exist in harmony and mutual pleasure are the homes where authority is clearly established.

How often do we need to establish our authority?

During the months when children begin walking, creeping, and getting into things, it is essential to establish authority repeatedly. In fact, it is a daily, even an hourly, struggle. Once it is firmly established, we can coast a little, with occasional checkpoints to assure both ourselves and the children that all is well—that God is in his heaven and that mama and daddy are still in charge.

Even though throughout their growing years, children continue to check dozens and even hundreds and thousands of times, and in as many ways, to see if we really mean what we say, they hope that we care enough to maintain the stands we take. They are not going to give us our authority as a gift—it is not theirs to give—yet they hope we will exercise that authority as an expression of our love for them. Otherwise, their world is not safe or secure.

When do we begin to establish authority over our children?

We need to establish parental authority from the beginning. How? By attending carefully, promptly, and lovingly to the needs of our infants, while at the same time letting them know that we cannot satisfy every want and relieve every discomfort; by letting them know that we are sympathetic, but not frantically eager to quiet every cry.

For example, at the age of five months, Mark learned to pull himself up to a standing position by holding onto the crib rail. When he discovered he did not know how to sit down again, he began to cry. His mother showed him repeatedly how to sit when he became tired, but he, like a jack-in-the-box, continued to pop back up. This frustrating routine lasted for several days, and it was only after his mother had let him cry several times that he finally realized that he could alleviate his own distress.

Who Is in Charge Here?

Won't my children think I am mean if I am the authority figure?

They will say so, especially when they want to break down your resistance so that you will give in on a decision.

What is an "authority figure" exactly?

Parents interact with their children in three basic styles—permissive, authoritarian, and authoritative (Baumrind. See Bibliography). *Permissive* parents, usually through efforts to be "nice," or through a belief that children should share in decision-making, do not establish parental authority.

Authoritarian parents take a do-what-I-say-because-I-say-it stance. This style often includes a lack of acceptance or understanding of children's needs, wants, and ideas.

Authoritative parents also make demands and rules, but they tend to set up boundaries and allow their children to operate within these boundaries—to make decisions and exercise their own wants and ideas. Baumrind's study indicates that children of permissive and authoritarian parents are often *less* responsive to parental desires and requests than are those of authoritative parents.

How do our children manage to get the upper hand?

Parents' guilt is the key to children's manipulation of them; children discover this at an early age. They learn a variety of ways to make us feel guilty about the rules we impose and the limits we set. Whatever our Achilles' heel, they find it. And once they do, they work on it. They learn to enlist the other parent in the struggle, or, if the parents are united, they hook grandparents, other relatives, babysitters, teachers, and friends into the game. They align whatever help is available, all the time hoping not to win.

What if parents don't present a united front?

Single parents find establishing and maintaining authority particularly difficult. Often a feeling of guilt about a divorce supplies additional leverage for their children and perhaps offers even greater opportunity to play one parent against the other. The single parent feels—and in many cases is—alone with this problem and the children. Not having the support and reality check of another adult in the household, they need to be particularly clear-headed about where their guilt (and married or divorced, we all have some) toward their children lies. When children see that the bases are covered—that we are not vulnerable at those points—then we, at least momentarily, have won the battle.

One way for parents, regardless of their circumstance, to avoid feeling wrong about imposing a rule, is to make sure that the rule is reasonable and that it is worth the trouble to enforce. Then enforce it. Then enforce it again.

How can we prepare, so that our teen-agers will not so totally reject authority?

Many parents feel that issues about authority do not come to a head until the teen-age years. Suddenly, from their point of view, pleasant, cooperative offspring become disagreeable rebels. Not since the toddler years and the "terrible twos" have the parents been told no at every turn. When reminded of those years, they say yes, but the kids were little and cute and didn't know better then. They are convinced that something beyond their control simply happened to their children (maybe they didn't have good teachers at school or maybe it's the gang of kids they hang out with) causing them to become suddenly—and unpredictably—hostile.

It is true that the teen-age years are, at best, perilous. Particularly during early adolescence, children may be their most unattractive and unappealing—and their most rebellious. They are awkward, uncertain, self-conscious, and difficult—trying to us and to themselves. The extent of turmoil varies from child to child, but they tend to be tumultuous years for most, to some degree. They will be unmanageable years, as well, if parental authority was not well established when they were younger. We can avoid many difficulties with our teen-agers by dealing fairly with them when they are young children, about such issues as their rights and privileges.

What rights are our children entitled to?

Children are human beings with feelings and rights of their own. This is surely obvious, yet many parents do not realize the implications of such a statement. They treat their children with less consideration, courtesy, and respect than they treat anyone else, even total strangers. They behave as though little kindnesses, simple good manners, and a sense of fair play apply to all relationships *except* those with their own children, where, undoubtedly, they matter most.

Legally, children have few rights in our society; their status in the courts traditionally has been about the same as that of property. In many families, this attitude is reflected in the treatment of their children; they are, in effect, chattel, with no rights of their own—no privacy, no ownership, no right to be heard, no right to innocence until proven guilty. Yet those who value children also value the rights children have, just by being children—the rights to health, education, protection, fair treatment in the courts and under the law—in short, the rights of full citizenship.

Children also have the right to our respect—for their feelings, needs, desires—and the right to childhood. Childhood, unlike private tutors and nursemaids, cannot be considered a luxury that few families can any longer afford and, consequently, something that children must learn to grow up without. Since humans are dependent longer than any other species, children *need* to be provided for and protected; otherwise, they will not survive. They have a right to dependency and protection, and having brought them into the world, we have no right to deny them what they need. They also will have many desires and make many demands of us throughout their growing up, and perhaps into adulthood, that we will be called upon to deny for their sake, as well as for our own, but their basic needs in order to survive and maintain their integrity as human beings must not be denied.

In the family of God, to be his child is to be given his kingdom, his name, access to his power—in short, the right to full membership in his family with his Son. As children of God, we share equal membership in the family of God with our children, and they with us.

Does this mean that our children are our equals?

No. In many ways, children are not our equals, and if we are to parent them properly, we must realize that. They are obviously not our equals in physical, intellectual, social, or emotional maturity, and they also are not our equals in spiritual and moral development. Maturation, of course, takes time, and children have not known the passage of very much time.

But there is something more distinctly different between the experiences and perceptions of adults and those of children than the simple fact that adults are older and wiser. The experiences and perceptions themselves are not the same. Children do not think as adults do; children do not perceive their surroundings objectively. Young children are self-centered and can view the world only from its center—themselves; they are incapable of seeing an incident from another person's viewpoint, and consequently, their demands are often selfish.

How can I tell the difference between the genuine needs my children have and the other demands they make?

The needs exhibited by children are numerous, incessant, and hard to distinguish from demands. We want to avoid "spoiling" our children, and equally important, we want to avoid ignoring genuine needs. We often find ourselves in a quandary when our children present a new request; is this a need or a demand—an effort to work us over? Parents must not assume that a fussy baby needs to cry for awhile before falling asleep unless they are certain a foot is not caught in the bars of the crib. They must not assume that a ten-year-old is deliberately not paying attention in class when he or she, in fact, is sick—or that a teen-ager is lazy when he or she is troubled or anxious. In order to distinguish needs from demands, parents must be closely attuned to their children and to what is going on with them at the time. Demands can be ignored successfully only when we are certain that needs are being met adequately.

Even when a genuine need exists, it is not always clear whether it is ours or theirs. This is one of the ways parents can help one another. When a child's need becomes confused with a parent's need, another parent may be able to lend a little perspective, another point of view. An example of this confusion can be seen often in the feeding patterns between mothers and babies.

During the early months of life most babies eat often, eagerly, and with satisfaction to themselves and to their mothers. After a few months the burst of growth lessens and so does a baby's appetite. But by this time, the mother's satisfaction in feeding has developed into a need. She feels rejected when the baby refuses food. She may invent games to distract the baby while getting one more spoonful of peas into the baby's mouth. The baby begins to notice that eating is very, very important to the mother and begins to play on this need of hers, perhaps learning to manipulate her through it. Manipulation may take the form of refusing to eat at mealtime, but demanding cookies, drinks, or other treats between meals. Then the mother begins to feel helpless; babies have to eat, don't they? It may take the form of drawing out this interaction concerning food, with both mother and baby spending more and more time in coaxing and wheedling. The mother coaxes and wheedles, trying to interest the baby in eating appropriate food in appropriate places at appropriate times, from her perspective. The baby coaxes and wheedles, trying the mother's patience and attempting to gain more attention, while eating less.

Who Is in Charge Here?

This cycle can be broken. How? Realizing that she is participating in a game that is increasingly frustrating to her and not helping the baby, the mother can decide to be hardhearted and uncaring about what, and whether, the baby eats. The baby won't believe her; there is too much accumulated evidence to show that she certainly does care—about every mouthful that does or does not go into the baby. If she can "play it straight" for three days, the cycle probably will be broken. If she can offer good food pleasantly, but without persuasion, at mealtimes for three days, the game-playing can be eliminated. If, even once during those three days, she engages in any of the repertoire of maneuvers that the baby has become used to, she will delay breaking up the game.

One lapse would cost another four or five days of diligent effort with no reinforcement, to extinguish the unwanted behavior. Psychologists call this random reinforcement. She would, by randomly engaging in the very thing she is trying to eliminate, reinforce it and make extinguishing the game and its manipulative behaviors much harder. Random reinforcement is the strongest type of reinforcement.

Another need/demand confusion occurs in relation to cleanliness. A need for cleanliness is usually the parent's need rather than the child's. Mothers often spend more effort and time on cleaning, washing, bathing, and wiping than most babies or children care about. Often those who keep children for parents are judged primarily, or feel themselves judged, by how clean the children appear. Pediatricians often say that most mothers clean children, particularly babies, too vigorously and unnecessarily, and that many parts of the body are self-cleaning, to some degree. As one suggests, we shouldn't put anything into any of the "holes" the baby has, except the mouth. Ears are supposed to have a protective wax, which rarely needs to be disturbed. Each of the other holes has a purpose, and the only one we need to poke anything into is the mouth.

Do I have the right to insist that my children pay attention to my needs?

Parents have needs, and we should be certain that, as parents, we own up to our needs and do not pass them off as belonging to our children. For instance, if we need our children to have high grades, then we must tell them that is our expectation and why, rather than pretending they need the As for their own reasons. Let them choose to seek grades to please us, rather than because we insist *they* need them.

But if the choice is up to them, they may not act responsibly.

That's true. But the choice is theirs anyway, regardless of what we do or do not say, although we can hope to bring some influence to bear. Besides, children can recognize whether or not we are being honest in our reasoning and can usually identify our real motivation. Most of the time, they will adhere to our genuine requests.

How can I help them to be responsible?

By letting them have responsibility. By allowing them opportunity to try things. By allowing them opportunity to fail. By allowing them opportunity to accept responsibility for their actions. By allowing them to experience the consequences of their actions whenever possible.

Who Is in Charge Here?

How can I let my children experience the consequences of their actions?

Allow them to make choices and live with those choices. Michael was a demanding four-year-old. One day he was told he could have an ice-cream cone at the end of a shopping trip, after all the errands had been completed. At the first stop, the dry cleaner had a gum machine, and he put up a howl for gum. He was told to choose gum now or an ice-cream cone later, after going to the bank and shoe shop. He chose gum immediately.

As he entered the ice-cream store a half hour later, he said, "I'll have chocolate." He was reminded that he had chosen gum. He promptly put the gum in a trash can and announced, "Chocolate." Even though he threw a temper tantrum, he did not get ice cream that day, but lived with the consequences of choosing gum.

But how do I decide who makes which choices at our house?

You decide on the basis of the consequences, both immediate and long-range. Letting our children make choices is a way of teaching them responsibility, but it is also a privilege that we grant, and we must protect them from making choices the consequences of which they cannot weigh or handle, should the worst happen. In determining who makes a decision, whether the choice involves which clothes our children wear or whether they go camping alone, we might do well to ask ourselves this question: If the worst possible happens, what are the ramifications to the children, to us as parents, and to the community? Can we live with the results of the child's choosing?

Sometimes I tell my children we are going to do something "my way" just because it is easier—not because it is an important decision. Am I being unfair?

No. Sometimes it makes sense to impose the parents' will on children, as a matter of convenience. There are many other times when parents make choices to suit the convenience of the children. It is when either the parents or the children must *always* give in to the convenience of the other that resentments accumulate.

Should I give my children as many choices as possible?

Most children need more genuine choices than they are offered, but to give unlimited or constant choices is to forget that children are sometimes faced with decisions that are too big for them, or more choices than they know how to handle. In today's world they are also faced with many choices that were not options a generation or two ago.

At every level of development children are relieved not to have to make *all* the choices and not to have to make *certain* choices. To be able to say "My folks won't let me" gets the teen-ager off the hook; to be able to say "My dad said not to do that" bails out a younger child.

How can I avoid tension when I allow my children to make choices?

Make sure that when offering a child a choice, a real choice is being offered. We may indicate to our children that they have some say in matters that we as parents have already decided in our own minds, or that we feel strongly must be handled in a certain way. We may ask, "Wouldn't you like to go see Aunt Louise this afternoon?" The children think they are being asked a real question: Do they or do they not want to go see their Aunt Louise? Then when they answer the question honestly and say no, we are irritated. We may even say blaming things, such as "You don't ever want to go see your Aunt Louise" or "You always make us go without you" or "You are selfish." The result is tension, hostility, and guilt feelings all around.

In this case, the children would have appreciated knowing from the outset where they stood and what was expected of them. If it was necessary to spend the afternoon doing something they did not want to do, they would have preferred to be told simply, "At three o'clock we are going to Aunt Louise's." Or if they are older and might be making plans of their own, they could have been forewarned, "Don't make any plans for Sunday afternoon because we are all going to Aunt Louise's."

Yes, but what if the children disagree with my decision?

First, we should make it clear that other options simply are not open. As parents, we can sympathize and understand; we may even agree with them and say quite honestly that there are other ways we would like to spend Sunday afternoon. By understanding and even agreeing, if we honestly can, we ally ourselves with them. More than getting their own way, what they probably want is acknowledgment of their point of view and understanding of their feelings. Then, when they go to Aunt Louise's anyway, we can show appreciation of their kindness and generosity, and they can experience the pleasure of having given something of themselves.

What are some examples of appropriate choices for young children?

Two-year-olds cannot be relied upon to choose anything in the closet to wear, but they can choose between two outfits. When their choices are respected, they will move on to making bigger and bigger choices.

Three-year-olds can be asked if they want lunch now. If they are given this choice and answer no, their answer must be respected. Adults often phrase directions to sound like choices; the real message may be, "Come to lunch." It may make sense simply to tell children to come to lunch; it does not make sense to ask if they are ready for lunch, when we mean for them to come and eat now.

Four-year-olds cannot accept the consequences of going into the street to play, but they can accept the consequences of choosing either gum at the beginning of a shopping trip or an ice cream at the end of it. This means that the parent who offers the choice must stand firm if the child chooses to put a penny in the gumball machine and hastily discard the gum as the ice-cream store is approached. There can be no giving in, if children are to begin to see and accept the consequences of their choices.

Many choices have to be made by parents or by other responsible adults to whom the parents give this responsibility. During the recent period of permissive child-raising, many parents became unsure about even giving their children appropriate directions. Some parents gave choices constantly, hoping not to frustrate or impose upon their own children the limits that had been imposed upon them as children. Instead of happy, creative, and productive people, however, the result was often frustrated, anxious, and obnoxious behavior. Parents who wanted so much to provide an atmosphere in which their children would bloom were hurt and mystified when the effect was the opposite of their expectation. When parents experience this kind of hurt, the result may be one of turning on the child. "What is the matter with you? I gave you all this good stuff and you are rude, rebellious, and don't even love me. What is the matter with you?" The child uses this hurt and guilt to manipulate more treats, favors, and freedom. But these are not actions that reassure the parent or the child that all is well—that they are God's children—that they are special.

Parents can make better choices for their children and take responsibility for them with less guilt if they have clear priorities for themselves and for their children. If their own and their children's relationship to God has first priority, the message the children receive will be clear and one that they can accept.

Will my children ever reach the age or maturity level when they can make all their decisions alone?

As long as they live in our house there will always have to be some joint decisions, even if our children are grown and married. For example, an eighteen-year-old legally can make the decision to marry, but most parents are not willing to permit even a child-of-age to marry and continue living at home with the same financial arrangement that existed until that time. This is not a decision the child should be allowed to make alone, because the consequences have ramifications that the parents probably won't want to live with.

Why all this emphasis on choices and who decides what?

Because this division of choices, or decisions, defines the difference between parents and children and the roles played by each. In recent years parents have become confused about who decides what, and both parents and children have been victimized by the resulting uncertainty and chaos. Unless we as parents can come to terms with the full responsibility of parenthood, as exemplified by dealing with the choices that are properly ours, we cannot hope to offer spiritual guidance of any consequence to our offspring.

How can I offer choices to my children and offer them guidance and discipline at the same time?

The kinds of choices we make available indicate to our children the guidance and discipline that we will provide for them. Unlimited choices indicate a lack of parental concern. Appropriate choices indicate guidance, caring, and discipline.

What is the aim of discipline?

It is to enable our children to become self-disciplined.

What kind of discipline is effective?

Many kinds of discipline are effective. What works best varies from parent to parent and from child to child, but the most effective discipline is an *atmosphere* established by the parents.

What do you mean by an "atmosphere" of discipline?

Who Is in Charge Here?

Each home has a climate unique to it and to its members. Children sense from this climate the kind of discipline that is imposed. In an atmosphere of mutual trust between adults and children, discipline problems are different from those in a home where there is suspicion and an expectation of wrong-doing. Children have a way of becoming what we say they are; this is the self-fulfilling prophecy. When we expect and predict the worst, that is what our children become. When we expect and prepare our children for self-discipline, they become self-disciplined.

But isn't "discipline" the same as "punishment"?

No. Punishment may be a part of discipline, and all children must probably at some time receive some type of punishment, but "discipline" means "to train," while "punish" means "to chastise."

Does discipline include spanking my children?

During the period from two to five years, an occasional spanking may be the best discipline—the best means of getting children's attention and letting them know that they must not do a particular act.

Is the period from two to five the only appropriate age to spank?

Children vary in the time they take to reach each level of maturity, but somewhere around the age of two, children begin to test the authority of their parents. Then a period of deliberate trying of the limits begins. At two, most children have developed a vocabulary that enables them to participate in verbal exhanges that have meaning, both to them and to their parents. At this time, when a verbal direction is ignored, a quick swat on the bottom serves as a reminder and deals with a minor irritation with dispatch.

If children are dealt with fairly, firmly, and consistently, by the age of five, or soon after entering school, most are more effectively punished by denying privileges than by spanking. Spanking older children humiliates and degrades both them and their parents, in a way that denial of privileges does not.

What can I do if I don't have the patience to discipline my children?

Even the most God-loving, God-fearing parents need an extra measure of patience, love, faith, strength, and fortitude, as they live through the years of their children's growing up. A greater patience than we ever thought possible can be a God-given gift to parents.

CHAPTER SIX

Training for Christian Living

Just as it is necessary to understand what children are like if we are to train them to be Christians, it is necessary to keep in mind the characteristics of Christians. By definition, a Christian is one who believes in the divinity of Jesus Christ and is blessed with the love, faith, and hope encompassed in that belief. We can teach our children to be good upstanding citizens and good moral people and omit the Christian message of Jesus Christ as the Son of God. We cannot, however, teach them to be Christians unless we raise them in a household where this message is central.

How can I train my children to serve?

As children begin to understand that they are gifts from God to their parents, they also begin to sense the commitment their parents have made to give them back to God. Over the years, this commitment becomes the children's own commitment to God. When we commit ourselves to something or someone, we seek ways to serve the cause or the person, and this concept also is true when commitment is made to

God. Though it is not possible to make a passive commitment to God, parents often speak the words of commitment for themselves and for their children without counting the cost. One cost of discipleship is service, but few parents actively teach their children to serve.

Servants in this democratic culture have almost disappeared. Service (and consequently a servant) has come to be held in low esteem. Many say they are "people-oriented" and want to "work with people," but few desire to work *for* others or to serve other people. Jesus said the first shall be last and the last shall be first; the greatest among us shall be least.

In our society of competition and aggressive self-seeking, the idea of serving has not been taught to very many children, although lip service may be paid to it. When they see conflict between what is said and what actually is lived-out before them, children react against their parents. Although we may give them mixed messages, they are astute readers of the real message—the one that controls us, rather than the one we say we believe.

Teaching children to serve seems to be the antithesis of helping them to feel good about themselves and to develop positive self-concepts. Teaching them to serve means teaching them quiet acceptance of themselves and others. It means teaching them to put others first and to find ways to put others' needs and desires before their own. Even the Lord's best friends, James and John, did not understand what it meant to serve Jesus. Their mother sought a place of honor for her sons on the right and the left of the Lord. But Jesus intended that they be servants—servants of God, servants to man.

In reality, this is an abhorrent ambition for most of

Training for Christian Living

us. We want more for our children. We may even teach them to be served, rather than to serve. Children whose parents serve them, pet them, and spoil them, are children who expect to be the center of attention. These are the children who are demanding and never satisfied, who cannot see the needs of others, and who always expect the biggest piece of cake, the first turn, and the special favor.

Hannah received Samuel as a gift from God and returned him to God. She taught him to serve; she gave him up; she put him in the temple where she could not serve his needs, but where she must trust in God that his needs would be met. Her mothering was reduced to providing a new coat once a year. A mother's greatest joy is in serving her children, and this makes it doubly hard for her to teach them to serve.

How are children taught to serve? Even a new baby can be taught to accommodate the family schedule. The more children there are, the more they usually adapt to the needs of the rest of the family. Parents of one or two children may not realize that even infants can learn to adapt. Some needs of infants must be met immediately and at odd hours of the day and night (feeding and diapering cannot wait), but it is not necessary for the entire schedule of the family to be determined by the baby.

As babies grow older, there are other ways they can be taught to serve. They can be taught that people other than parents can be trusted, and they can learn to stay happily with other people. This is not something they will think up for themselves; they must be taught.

Toddlers can be allowed to "help"—to pick up toys, dust, even wash dishes. It is easier to pick up toys, dust, and especially wash the dishes ourselves, but if we let children in on a task early, while they are toddlers and while they still think of it as a game, they will learn to serve. The time when they decide this is not fun will come quickly, but children who are allowed to participate in what adults are doing will move on with the adults to new tasks, learning new ways to serve. Often a problem arises from having denied toddlers the opportunity to participate. Later, when they are really big enough to help, it may be too late to have happily participating youngsters.

As children mature they also can be taught to serve by learning to wait. Much of school and other living is waiting. In our eagerness to provide "fun" for our children we take on the role of tour guide or entertainer. Neither of these roles helps to teach service.

By teaching our young children to accommodate the schedule of others, to stay with caring adults other than their parents, to "help" before they are really able to help, and to wait courteously, we are teaching them to serve even before the concept can be grasped. And, as in most things we teach our children, they will model what they see us do. If we serve God and others joyously and naturally, our children will expect to serve also. They will do what they see us doing.

As children take on tasks to help their parents, they need help in learning how to do those tasks. Parents very often extend this help in the form of criticism, "I just want it done right!" When children see the bed they just made remade, the floor remopped, or the windows gone over again, the clear message they receive is one of being inadequate. In letting children help with the cooking, for example,

Training for Christian Living

we need to value the children more than the dish being prepared. It will help to remember that the children are also being prepared, and that they are more important.

First efforts at sewing, cooking, driving, mowing, washing, and so on, often leave something to be desired. Though it is not a favor to children to accept sloppy efforts repeatedly, it is necessary to accept first efforts as first efforts. When we teach another adult to perform a task, we offer encouragement, congratulations, and even help them to finish. Our children certainly deserve as much. Too often they do not receive the same courtesy and help that our friends, colleagues, and even casual acquaintances are offered. We first accept our friends as people, and then we gratefully accept their service in whatever form they want to give it; as our children offer service to us and to others, they deserve support, help, and appreciation. They translate lack of positive response to mean that they are not accepted and thus are reluctant to offer help again.

One of the difficult things to learn is that genuine service occurs only when we have met the needs of another. What others need is often not what we need to give; we frequently try to serve by giving what we want others to receive, rather than by meeting their real need. Children can be taught to tune in to another's needs in such a way that true service will be the outcome.

How can I teach my children to worship?

Jesus said, "Let the children come to me; do not try to stop them" (Matt. 19:14 NEB). Before children are able to talk, move about independently, object or reject, is the time to begin to bring them to God. If we wait until they can understand, cooperate, and show interest, we wait too long. Participation in worship —the rite of showing reverence, the acting out of intense love and admiration—is one of the ways we bring our children to God. At a very early age children are ready to learn what worship is.

Before children can talk they begin to sort out what fits, what is appropriate, what is like, and what is unlike. For instance, Anna could scarcely sit securely alone before she sorted through a dish of smooth stones, carefully setting aside each one until she came to a small piece of driftwood. It clearly did not fit; she tossed it away. Later when she was about two, she loved to stand on a sturdy crate and "wash" dishes. She would engage in water play, using sponge, suds, and a variety of kitchen objects, as long as an adult could tolerate her use of the sink. She quickly learned to be careful with breakable dishes and carefree with plastic ones. This ability to identify *likes* and *differences* is essential for later reading skill—noting the difference between A and B, "saw" and "was."

This skill is also related to development of the spiritual discernment involved in worship. As young children participate in worship experiences with others, the same process of becoming aware of what is appropriate, what fits, is taking place. Children become aware that there are periods of quiet, rejoicing, sadness, and remorse, as others relate to God. During their first two years children are not even sure where they begin and end, or where their parents begin and end. The sense of self is so undefined and the attachment to parents so strong that children feel a part of their parents and a part of whatever the parents are doing.

Training for Christian Living

While children are still sorting sticks from stones, breakable from unbreakable, self from others, is the time to begin to share worship with them. Worship may be in a church service, in songs that reflect a love for God, in family prayers, or in the parents' individual prayers that children observe and respect as time spent with God—a time not to be interrupted with trivial things. None of these do young children "understand," but these acts of worship build their relationship with God before they understand there is any choice about that relationship.

The dependence of young children makes sharing all aspects of our own worship—prayer and celebration of life—possible and almost necessary. In modern households parents find it difficult to exclude the very young from these acts of devotion.

Parents, of course, need time and space away from their children, and children need some time and space away from their parents. Perhaps parents must even get away completely from time to time for prayer and spiritual renewal; Christ himself often withdrew into the wilderness to pray and seek God.

Christ also often took the disciples with him for support and training, although they frequently could not grasp what he was about, and he was disappointed in their inability to pray for long periods, as he did. They often did not understand what he was teaching; they asked questions he thought he had answered, and others that hurt him because he hoped they had grown beyond such concerns; they often focused on aspects of the kingdom that were not important. In other words, they often behaved like little children. In spite of these behaviors and lack of understanding, he continued to take the disciples with him—to the temple, to quiet places of prayer, as he taught the multitudes, as he served, as he was honored, as he was reviled, as he celebrated weddings, feasts, burials, and life. As the disciples followed him, not understanding, questioning, and competing, he was teaching them what they would need to know after he was gone. He was preparing them to function without his physical presence. He was also teaching them to accept suffering, ridicule, hardship, and deprivation, and to live by tenets of a personal philosophy that was beyond their grasp. In order to prepare them, he spared them very little; he shared his triumphs and his degradation.

Even when our children are very young, we can and must share the real stuff of living—the hurts, disappointments, fears, joys, successes, and triumphs. We are not doing them a favor when we spare them hardship and give them a pablum diet; we will only wonder later why they see no strength in service, find no comfort in faith, and order their priorities so that God is left out of their lives.

This does not mean parading all our sins and temptations before our children or imposing on them a burden of fear, but usually children are sensitive to their parents' feelings and know when there is hurt, trial, or joy. By sharing a willingness to let God solve our problems, we allow our children to see our own dependence on him and our expectation of depending on his day-to-day help. This should lead them to expect God's help and to expect to depend on him. In this way children grow to believe that dependence is strength, not weakness.

How can I train my children to praise?

As special gifts to God, we commit ourselves to him, we serve him, and we give him praise. In our praise we express an awareness of well-being and an appreciation for being well loved and cared for. Praise also releases us to receive gifts from God, and it enables us to join with the hosts on high in the adoration that is continually before the throne. God has commanded that we praise him. It helps to tie us to him, and also enables us to declare ourselves one with him.

Children learn to praise by being praised. They know they are loved when they are told they are loved and when they are praised. Jesus told his disciples that the Scriptures say, "Even little babies shall praise him" (Matt. 21:16). When Jesus taught his disciples to pray, he began and ended the brief prayer with praise. We can teach our children prayers of praise and songs of praise in the same way and, by so doing, help them to develop a deeper understanding of God. Praise is an integral part of becoming a gift to God.

How can I train my children to pray?

Prayer is related to praise. But prayer is communication *with* God, not just *to* God. It is receiving, as well as sending messages—listening, as well as petitioning the Almighty. By praying with our children and teaching them to pray, we help them increase their trust relationship with the Father.

Prayer evokes guilt in many adults because we feel inadequate about how we pray or that we do not pray as often as we should or that God seems so remote that praying seems a waste of time and effort. A meaningful prayer life takes time; a meaningful relationship with others takes time. God is no exception; it takes time to know him and to communicate with him. Often we feel disappointed with ourselves and with God because we feel out of touch with him. Communication is cut off by our being too busy, too self-sufficient, and too selfish. When we can get along in life by ourselves, we don't need God. When we are ego-centered, and not God-centered, there is little real communication. When we are brought to our knees because we cannot find our own answers and because there is no one else who meets our needs, then communication with God can occur. That is not a place we willingly choose for our children, nor is it a place we choose for ourselves; it is the place where we must be if we are to reach out and find God.

We teach prayer to our children just as we teach many other things—by doing it with them. Often we are self-conscious and vague as we pray, but our children deserve to see us in real communication with God. This means letting our children see us confess mistakes, sins, weaknesses, and the need for help; it means letting our children see us ask for help with big and little problems; it means letting our children see us expect, recognize, and accept God's answers, and live by them.

How can I train my children to give?

When we allow our children to become demanding, greed results, and they refuse to share their possessions or family responsibilities. When this occurs, they are perceiving love to be in short supply—be it in the form of our time, attention, or affection—or that some of life's basic comforts, such as food, warmth, or privacy, are insufficient. They begin to compete for whatever seems to be limited, and we may even encourage this selfishness and competition by teaching them to hold on to what they have.

Children learn to be generous by observing that we are generous with them and with others. Regardless of what we say to them about generosity, if they see us selfish and grasping, they do not believe the message we tell them, but the message we show them.

Children cannot learn how to share what is theirs without first understanding the concept of ownership. They can be taught at an early age to distinguish between what is theirs and what belongs to someone else. Though this is a simple concept, we often give our children mixed messages about ownership. For example, we may say "Don't play with my things" or "Don't borrow my things without permission," and then we pick up the unfinished sandwich off their plate at lunchtime and eat it, or take their toys and loan them to others, or give their old belongings away—all without asking their permission.

If we want them to respect the belongings of others, then we must respect their belongings. Even two-year-olds want the assurance that no one is going to eat the food off their plates or take the toys out of their toy chests without asking if it is all right with them.

Most young children delight in sharing their toys when they sense they will return to them. Even babies enjoy thrusting an object into someone else's hands, only to snatch it back again. Possession must be learned in order for sharing to take place.

Children learn to share in chores and responsibilities by having their parents share with them. When parents are clear possessors of the stereo, for instance, children feel privileged to learn to use it properly. Children who respect the property of others in the family can learn to ask permission to borrow from one another and to care for the borrowed item. They in turn will be willing to share their own property.

Considerations of privacy are very like those of ownership. We expect our children to respect our privacy, whether it is the closed bedroom door, the half-hour of peace and quiet with the evening paper, or the uninterrupted telephone conversation. We, in turn, must respect theirs, whether it is the whispered secret with playmates, the diary hidden under the pillow, or the personal letter from a friend.

Once these rights of ownership and privacy are clearly established for both parents and children, then sharing can become a real privilege. When children know that if they say Andy cannot play with their trucks or that Mary cannot play with their dolls, that Andy or Mary won't be permitted to do so; then they can have the pleasure of being generous and sharing if they choose, and if they choose not to share, they soon realize the pleasure they are missing. Of course, when they also know from experience that Andy breaks trucks and Mary refuses to return dolls, they are spared anxiety by knowing that they have the right—and that the right will be granted to them—to say no.

Also, once the right to privacy has been established as belonging to both children and adults, children are willing to be more generous and understanding about their parents' need for closed doors, uninterrupted time, and peace and quiet. Children need to know that, just because we are parents, we do not assume we have the right to eavesdrop, snoop, or pry.

Training for Christian Living

All children, because they are children, enjoy secrets, and all children, because they are human beings, need a certain amount of privacy. If opportunity for privacy is not willingly granted, then they may feel forced to seek it in ways that draw suspicion and create guilt.

In even the most open relationship between parents and children, there usually arise some occasions when we are concerned that our children are deliberately keeping something from us and that they are troubled. We have the responsibility to say just that to them—that we do not know what is on their mind or why they are behaving in certain ways, but that we have noticed they appear upset or worried. Then we offer to help. If a trusting relationship has already been established, our children probably will choose to confide in us. However, they may choose to do so on their own time schedule, not ours, and we may be called upon to wait until they are ready to talk. In the meantime, we should not go behind their back to find out what is troubling them.

In teaching our children to give, we need to remember that in Old Testament days, God asked his people for the first fruits of their harvests. A key to cheerful giving still is to give of the first fruits, rather than after all debts are paid and all necessities cared for. The first daisies of spring are full of promise; the first produce from the garden is an indication of the plenty to follow. Children can learn to give the first of whatever is available, whether it is cookies they help bake, shells they find on the shore, or the first colorful leaves of autumn.

Children also can be taught that the best of what they do is a gift for God. Because they are very like the rest of us, children look for the acceptable level of production, and then are apt to deliver at that level. They quickly notice whether they are allowed to offer slipshod work or whether they are pushed to do their best. When adults compliment children on tasks done or pictures drawn or stories told that the children know are hardly their best efforts, then they conclude that the adults are not really paying much attention. This is hardly a compliment, and even young children know it. To be overly praised for something that is easy does not make children feel good about the way the task was done or about the adult who does the praising. On the other hand, when both children and adults acknowledge that a task is hard and that it has been well accomplished, the praise is real, and a best effort has been recognized.

CHAPTER SEVEN
Dealing with Moral Problems

Children do not come into the world to cause problems, but as parents, we sometimes feel we run from one problem to another, and that parenthood offers little but a series of fires to be put out. The magnitude of the problem depends, in part, on what we expect and how we react. The emphasis in this chapter is on handling problems in early childhood; the difficulties later will be influenced by how well the problems are handled when they first arise.

What can I do when my children lie?

All children lie sometimes. At least, upon occasion, they all tell us something more, or less, or altogether different from, the facts. They do not always do this in order to deceive us, however. Very young children (before school age) may lack a clear differentiation between reality and fantasy. They may "lie" to make a good story or a convincing point. They may tell us, for example, that their teddy bear has gone on a trip or that their imaginary playmate is having his tonsils out. These "lies" are told for the same reasons that adults brag and exaggerate.

When children tell tall tales, parents can acknowledge them as just that—good stories. There is no need to pin them down by asking if they are telling the truth, but we can let them know we don't believe the stories without labeling them "liar."

It is important to remember that most labels are not useful between parents and children, particularly a label such as liar, often said in a tone devastating to children.

Because young children confuse reality and fantasy, they need adult help in distinguishing between the two. Frequently adults add to this perplexity by answering questions in a flip manner. Some questions from children are complex, and we may not know the answers. Or, particularly when the questions are constant and repetitive, we do not want to take the trouble to give a complete answer. So children sometimes are told such things as "It's magic" or "A little man who lives inside the refrigerator turns on the light." Is it any wonder children make up stories of their own?

When parents give serious consideration to what their children say to them and to their reply, an expectation of truth and belief is established. To tell an untruth is a breach of trust, when a trusting relationship has been assured. Most children *want* to tell the truth to trusted parents and other adults.

Parents also often set the stage for their children's lies by telling lies themselves. Sometimes these are told because the children are young and gullible, and the lie saves bother—"There's not enough time to play ball before dinner." When children know there is an hour before dinner, they quickly translate this into, "I want to do something else besides play ball with you." In this way, children are taught distrust, and in time, they themselves may begin to lie.

Dealing with Moral Problems

How much better to say, "I want to read the paper now, but we will play ball after dinner." Of course, this answer is truthful only if ball playing does occur after dinner. All too often the promise is not kept, and so children are taught another way to lie—by not keeping promises.

Older children may lie to protect themselves. Frequently parents push them to lie by threatening such severe punishment the children feel they must lie. Parents may know the answer, but push a child to admit wrongdoing by asking, "Did you break the lamp?" or even "Why did you break the lamp?" Such questions are not really questions, but accusations. A more effective approach is to offer to help clean up the pieces and to ask sympathetically, "How did it happen?" If another adult broke a lamp, most people would react in this manner, offering help and sympathy, rather than accusations. When we extend the same courtesy to our children that we offer to our friends, many problems between parents and children are averted.

Sometimes we may know that our children have lied to us, although we may not know for what reason. When we come upon evidence that this is the case, we do not need to tempt them to lie again by asking them to verify the facts. However, we do need to let them know that we realize they have lied to us and that we are disappointed. If we are scrupulously honest in all our dealings, especially those with our children, such behavior is not likely to occur more than a time or two. Then it usually happens regarding some experimental activity in early adolescence of which they are ashamed.

If children are to learn to tell the truth, they must be listened to sympathetically and trustingly at every age. Unless there is some clear and specific reason to doubt what they say, we should not question them. When we say aloud, "I wonder if that's so" about something a young child says or when we quiz an older child in a skeptical way, the clear message they receive is that we do not believe what they say. They then decide—which is obviously the case—that it makes no difference whether they lie or tell the truth, because we do not believe them in any event. By accepting what they say without question, we can show them that we also accept *them* without question.

What can I do when my children steal?

Most children will take something that is not theirs even after learning it is wrong to do so, and they need to learn to live with the consequences. Early instances of this behavior usually occur in a store or in a neighbor's house or yard. Young children will usually let their parents know they have something for which they did not pay or ask. The question, then, is what to do about the pack of gum from the store or the knickknack from the neighbor's coffee table found in their hand or pocket. Parents may lecture, scold, look shocked, laugh it off, do nothing, or feel ashamed. None of these responses does much to change the child's behavior or to keep stealing from occurring again. The most useful response is to explain calmly that the gum or other object really belongs to someone else and then to go with them to return it or to offer payment and apology. When this is done immediately, children sense the importance of returning the object and admitting the mistake. If prompt restitution occurs, little more needs to be made of the incident, as they

Dealing with Moral Problems

will see clearly the importance to us of making the situation right. Then whether the storekeeper or the neighbor is angry or rewarding is of small consequence.

One such incident may be enough to establish clearly that we disapprove, and that stealing is wrong. If it happens again we need to repeat the procedure of going with our children to return the object and face the adults involved.

If children of any age have money, toys, clothes, or other things that we did not provide, we need to find out where they came from or from whom, and our children, in turn, need for us to notice these things, as well as to notice what they are doing. Inquiries of this sort should not be couched in suspicious or accusing language, but voiced as simple questions, which we, as parents, have the right to ask. Whatever the explanation, we do not need to seize on the occasion to moralize or to preach a sermon. If the objects do not seem to be in our children's possession rightfully, we should react much as we did when they were younger, immediately helping them to return the things and offering apology or restitution to the owners. Shaming our children with comments—"You are old enough to know better"—or by labeling them "thief" only creates guilt and resentment and is not useful in changing their behavior—except to make them more secretive.

We also need to be aware of our own behavior. Just as our children learn truthfulness by hearing us tell the truth, they learn attitudes about taking what is not theirs in the same way. Adults who would not dream of shoplifting, for example, may not hesitate to put an ashtray from a restaurant table into their pocket or towels from a motel room into their suitcase. They may also brag about getting the best of someone in a business deal or getting away with something on their tax return. There is no reason to think that children see these activities in any light other than what they are—taking something that rightfully belongs to someone else. If what we say does not agree with what we do, then our children cannot trust us.

Older children who steal are probably in some sort of troubled situation they cannot handle alone, and by stealing and getting caught, they are in fact asking for help. They are saying to us, "Tune in. Look at me. I am not old enough, or wise enough, or strong enough to handle the life I am living. Help me." How we can help depends upon the situation, but we cannot afford to ignore this plea or postpone our response. We may need to seek professional counseling, as well as moral support from those who love us and our children. And seeking help may be all the more difficult because of our own shame and ego involvement.

What can I do when my children cheat?

Children cheat when the task they are expected to accomplish or the grade they are expected to achieve seems impossible. We can help by taking off the pressure for perfection. By accepting a less-than-perfect performance, or a lower grade, we show our children that we prefer less, earned honestly, to more, gained dishonestly.

When they are caught cheating, we should explain the worth of honest effort and go with them to make right anything that needs to be corrected. We can assure them that we know cheating is not their usual practice and that we expect good things from them.

Dealing with Moral Problems

We also need to make sure we are not giving them a mixed message—verbal affirmations of honesty and behavioral examples of cheating. Whether in figuring our income tax, going through the grocery check-out line, or relating to our spouse, we need to set continual examples of honesty. Even such an incident as asking our children to lie to someone on the phone by saying we are not at home, serves as a message that we do not *really* mean what we say about being aboveboard in all our dealings.

What can I do when my children are secretive?

They will be—and they ought to be—about certain things at certain times. We are not supposed to know their every thought, and we could not, even if we would. From the beginning, each child is a separate entity with an individual identity and his or her own way of relating. As parents, we can only know our children from our own relationship with each one, not from their relationship with anyone else—even their other parent. As young children, they will sometimes relate to grandparents, brothers and sisters, and other relatives and friends in a way that excludes us. If we encourage other relationships from the beginning, they will grow up sharing secrets and experiences with others in a way that is healthy and beneficial for them and for us.

As they grow and experience more and more of life away from our scrutiny, we must rely on them to share with us what they choose. In order for them to share *very much* with us, we must listen attentively and be truly interested, rather than distracted or probing. Even then, they will select and monitor what they want us to know. If we share important feelings and decisions with them, they will be more likely to share significant, rather than mundane, aspects of themselves with us.

When we have a close relationship with our children, we may be alarmed if they suddenly appear secretive, and we need to be alert to what such signals may mean. Are they testing to see if we will let them have secrets? Or are they letting us know they are carrying a heavy burden? Is there something they want us to know without their telling us? We must take care not to ignore signals of distress and trouble, in the name of permitting privacy. They always need our concern about their well-being; they can do without our idle curiosity about their secrets—thanks just the same.

What can I do when my children are rude?

We owe our children lessons in courtesy to make them bearable to others. Teaching them to be polite includes teaching consideration of others—and this means more than saying please and thank you. Some of the rudest people use conventionally polite terms. Truly gracious behavior means putting others first—doing unto others as you would have them do unto you. Showing good manners is simply acting out the Golden Rule. Children must be taught this, and in order for them to learn, they must be treated with consideration themselves and see us treat others with consideration. This means that we must take the time and effort to do for others, so that our children may learn by our example.

What can I do when my children disobey me?

They will—sometimes. As children of God, all of us disobey sometimes. Just as God accepts and loves us

Dealing with Moral Problems

when we disobey, we need to accept and love our children when they disobey.

Appropriate response to disobedience depends on the child's maturity, whether this is the first incidence of this type of disobedience, and whether we are dealing with a hard-to-manage or an easy-to-manage child. In his book *Infants and Mothers: Differences in Development,* T. Berry Brazelton suggests that infants can be designated as average, quiet, or active, even at the time of birth. Psychologists Chess and Thomas report nine types of temperament evident at birth, in *Temperament and Behavior Disorder in Children.* Although fundamental rules and acceptable behavior within a family may be agreed upon, some adjustments must be made to accommodate each individual child. Just as all children are not alike, they do not all need to be treated alike. Indeed, they *must* not be treated exactly alike if each is to receive the nurturing and training he or she most needs.

Parents also have differing temperaments—distinct from that of each child and from each other. Consequently, each one-on-one relationship within the family has characteristics of its own.

Regardless of temperaments and combinations of temperaments in a household, it is important to have as few "laws" as possible and to say yes, unless there is a very good reason not to. And once we have "laid down a law," we must take the trouble to make it stick, unless, of course, we realize we have made a mistake. Then we need to remove the law from the books and tell our children right away that we were wrong.

Whenever possible, we need to let our children know ahead of time what is expected of them. When we set reasonable, enforceable standards and show them what we expect, obedience is a reasonable expectation. *Then,* if they disobey, we need to work to change their behavior.

In order to do this, it may be necessary to punish, but we should keep in mind that our goal is obedient and, eventually, self-disciplined children. Self-discipline, not punishment, is the objective. If behavior can be changed by punishment, then punishment can be measured by using the least possible required to correct a particular act of disobedience by a particular child.

An easy-to-manage child will require guidance, suggestion, a good model, and very little else in order to become an attractive, responsive person. A hard-to-manage child may require close supervision, limited choices, specific punishments for specific infractions, and still be difficult. Take heart—some children simply outgrow being hard to manage. Some parents learn techniques that work, and difficulties lessen as time goes by. Some parents manage better when their children are young; some do better when their children are older.

What can I do when my children are tattletales?

Usually adults make children into tattletales by asking for information about a sibling's whereabouts or activities. Even when we do not elicit this response children are easily encouraged by our interest in the information they have to offer and are quick to jump into this role.

As adults, we tend to expect to play referee and arbitrate squabbles. It is a rare adult who does not succumb to initiating "Big Brother is watching you" and an even rarer adult who fails to respond to

Dealing with Moral Problems

"Johnny took my tricycle." Children fuel the fire by getting their brothers, sisters, and friends in trouble with parents or other adults, whenever they are displeased with their playmates' behavior.

The quick and effective method for putting an end to tattling is to be disinterested in the tale. Respond with nothing, "Oh," or "Don't you like it when someone takes your blocks? Then don't tell me, tell Johnny you don't like it." Even three-year-olds quickly grasp the message that they are to deal directly with each other, rather than run to an adult to solve the problem.

When we fail to respond, tattling is quickly done away with, especially when children face each other with negative feelings. A child who teases or bullies is stopped by other children more quickly than by adults. Moreover, if an adult responds to each infraction or hurt, the offender is receiving attention that may cause repetition of negative behavior.

What can I do when my children hurt and bully other children?

Children learn early to take advantage of one another. They usually bully or tease weaker children when they feel put down or incompetent themselves, much as we may try to bolster ourselves by putting down someone else. So just when our children are the most unlovable and most unloving, they need to be loved the most.

In addition to loving them and spending time that focuses on them, we may need to separate them from other children. As soon as either physical or emotional hurting behavior begins, we can say, "No, you must not do that," and remove them from the situation. For young children, this may be a brief separation of a few minutes; for older children, it may be for a longer period. After a brief explanation, the children should be separated immediately. It is usually not necessary to scold or otherwise punish. Most children want to be with other children, and the denial alone is deterent enough.

What can I do when my children are quarrelsome?

Are you quarrelsome? Notice whether you contradict your children, your mate, or your friends. If your children see you disputing and disagreeing with much of what is said, they will, too; but if they see you being forthright and honest in a pleasant and agreeable manner, they will learn to voice differing opinions in a pleasant and agreeable way, too.

If your children have already established a habit of being contentious, how quickly you can help them to change is remarkable to watch. When they dispute something that is said, reply, "Do you think so?" or "You may be right." They will be startled at first when they fail to receive an argumentative response in turn, but soon they will begin to imitate your pleasant way of giving the other person the benefit of the doubt.

If your children fight among themselves—and they will if they are near in age—let them work out their own problems whenever possible. You may need to intervene if an older child takes advantage of a younger one, but let them know that, in general, you do not intend to referee. Of course, for your own sanity and perhaps even for their safety, you may need to separate them for a cooling-off period occasionally, but permitting them to tattle to you and to expect you to monitor their behavior tends to

Dealing with Moral Problems

alienate them from one another and, eventually, from you.

What can I do when my children are jealous?

All children are jealous at times; it is part of the human condition, but jealousy can be minimized. Here are some suggestions.

1. Remember, the more carefully we measure to assure equal treatment, the more apt they are to complain—"His cookie is bigger." "She's always first." "Why do I always have to give in?"

2. Do try to treat each child fairly.

3. Do not prefer one child over another.

4. Love each child's special qualities, even the idiosyncracies.

5. Say words of love to each child.

6. Show affection in loving ways that each child can accept.

Logan Wright, author of *Parent Power: A Guide to Responsible Childrearing,* points out that each child's variance in style calls for consideration in showing love. A grandmother who insists on kissing a baby, a six-year-old granddaughter, and an eleven-year-old grandson in the same way on each visit is punishing at least one of the three children—and all three might prefer another type greeting.

Different families put premiums on different characteristics—beauty, talent, grades, athletic ability, musical performance. Children who feel unable to measure up to the family standard may feel jealous, afraid, and unsure of themselves.

CHAPTER EIGHT

The Place of Ritual and Doctrine in Spiritual Training

As parents, we give our children many messages, and the clearest of these lie in what we do, not in what we say. Ritual offers us the opportunity to act out expressions of faith with our children. And with each repetition, we experience faith made manifest, mystery made manageable, and we and our children are bound closer to God. Doctrine, the intellectual approach to faith, then follows—in its own time.

What part does ritual play in spiritual training?

Ritual defines who is, and who is not, a member of a group, whether that group be a family, a church, or some other. Because ritual is satisfying only when it is familiar and when we are included in it, unfamiliar ritual causes us to feel set apart and lonely. Acquaintance with its rituals can introduce us to an understanding of a group, but only ritualized behavior of our own, derived from active participation and long-term practice, assures us that we belong.

Ritual provides a means of anticipation and is full of promise. Whether it is the hanging of the

The Place of Ritual and Doctrine

Christmas stockings, grace said before dinner, or the rite of Holy Communion, ritual is done in expectation of something to come and thus is an acting out of hope and faith.

The practice of ritual—that daily, weekly, or yearly "acting out" of a prescribed form—grounds our faith and expands our spiritual perimeters. Ritual offers us a way to discover our spiritual selves; it is not the sum of our faith, but the vessel in which we elect to keep it. Without faith, ritual is dry and empty, but without ritual, faith is scattered and uncontained. When faith runs dry, ritual continues, and out of its continuation, faith can be renewed. When ritual is disrupted, faith will seek expression until ritual is reestablished.

At what age should we begin to include our children in rituals?

As soon as they are born.

But what do they gain from rituals they don't understand?

Repetition is an important part of all learning, and ritual offers repetition as a means to spiritual learning and growth. Ritual begins to build faith even before teaching can establish belief and inform understanding. Examination of the meaning of the rituals can teach lessons about the family or the church, but it is the repetition that trains behavior and shapes development. As we stake a young plant so that it will grow upright, ritual straightens us when we are young and flexible and directs our desire for belief and our striving for faith, out of which growth takes place.

But what if we don't have any family rituals?

You do. All families have rituals, although they may not be recognized as such and may be little more than habits that, over a period of time, have become imbued with some sort of meaning.

What are some examples of rituals that both children and adults find meaningful?

Daily rituals tend to center around the dinner table and bedtime because these are times, and often the only times, when parents and children are routinely together. Out of these daily routines, habits are bound to evolve, and patterns, whether pleasant or unpleasant, rewarding or punishing, are created. These patterns offer an ideal opportunity for ritualized activities that the entire family will find meaningful and a source of comfort and encouragement. Family prayers can be said at the table, and bedtime rituals, particularly important to young children, can include stories and songs, as well as prayers.

Should these table and bedtime rituals be religious?

Why not? These are ideal times to begin to train our children to incorporate religion into their daily lives.

But what if I am not comfortable with religious ceremonies outside of church?

These intimate family rituals do not need to be performed in the manner of big ceremonies. They can be as simple or as elaborate as feels appropriate for the circumstance and comfortable for the family involved. They are our own—of our own making,

The Place of Ritual and Doctrine

originating out of our own belief, performed out of our own faith. They may be, according to our preference, age-old prayers or blessings handed down for centuries in our church or family litany; they may be simple prayers in some family member's words; they may be stories, new or old, read or told, that are repeated within the family circle until they come to symbolize the uniqueness of our family. They may even be symbolic gestures—the sign of the cross, the hand laid on a child's head in blessing, the head bowed or the knee bent in prayer. The solemnity or informality of the ritual will depend on what each family finds comfortable.

What other occasions are suitable for rituals?

Holidays and family celebrations have traditionally been times of special rituals. Ritual adds suspense and drama, as well as a sense of continuity and dependability to these occasions, and children rejoice in it. The excitement of Christmas, the joy of Easter, the special importance of a birthday—these are gifts we bring our children through ritual. Each family develops its own version of these occasions, and the children themselves may expand the rituals.

What about the rituals of the church? At what age do children begin to participate in them?

Like the rituals at home, the rituals of the church hold excitement for children. There also they find suspense and drama, a sense of continuity and dependability. Some churches, of course, are more highly ritualized than others, but all churches have rituals, and children of all ages can participate to some degree. What the rituals are, and what part children play in them, vary greatly from church to church, but children should not be relegated entirely to the nursery or left at home until they are old enough to understand their meaning. As much as possible, they should be included in the rituals of both the home and the church, from the time they are born.

But what good does it do them to participate before they can understand what is going on?

Ritual offers opportunity for training, and as with other kinds of training, it involves a sharing of experience between parents and children, the revelation of ourselves to one another and, in the case of religious ritual, to God. Out of this revelation comes heightened self-awareness, and we become more centered within ourselves, more consciously connected with one another and with God. Even before children can grasp or question intellectually the meaning of the rituals, they can be included in the spiritual environment where these mysteries are found. This is one way we welcome them into the Christian communion and introduce them to the universal aspects of the Christian experience.

But don't we have to teach them Christian beliefs?

Yes, we have to teach them, but lessons in the tenets of the Christian doctrine will have little meaning unless they are taught in conjunction with training of which ritual is a part. *Training* begins with birth, but *teaching* begins when they are ready, and they will let us know. There is no point in trying to teach a six-month-old baby the ABCs, but in a few years, you can scarcely keep a bright child from learning not only the alphabet, but how to read.

The Place of Ritual and Doctrine

Young children will simply accept without question, not only our rituals, but our faith. Their nature is not to question, but to trust. When they are older they will realize that all people don't participate in the same rituals, but that there are many different ones. Then they will ask why.

Do you mean we don't need to offer any explanations until we're asked?

Yes, but that's not to say our children won't ask *any* questions before they are old enough to begin searching out theological explanations. From the time they can talk, they question us continually about everything we do and say, and religious and spiritual matters are no different. In fact, children are particularly curious about religious rituals because they are so rich in drama and suspense. "Why are you lighting those candles?" or "What's in that cup?" or "What are they doing with that water?" provide us many teaching opportunities, but we need to be careful that our answer consists of information our children want to know and are ready to learn. Teaching about God and religion is similar to teaching about other difficult subjects, such as sex or death. With such subjects, children frequently do not get the answers they need when they need them, and they do not always get their answers from the most desirable or reliable sources. When a five-year-old asks, "What's in the cup?" that is probably exactly what he or she wants to know, and a simple answer of "wine" will probably be the most satisfactory. An opportunity for theological teaching about communion symbols is still a long way off, although no doubt it will come in time. If the simple, direct response does not satisfy the child's curiosity, his or her further questions will invite us to offer a fuller explanation. As time goes by and our children grow older, their questions will become more sophisticated and more complicated.

Should we send them to Sunday school?

Yes, if the Sunday school serves to reinforce their positive feelings about the church, and about themselves in relation to the church, as well as offering them a good learning experience.

We should choose a Sunday school with the same care we would choose any other school. Just as different children benefit from different types of schools, they also benefit from different Christian education opportunities. For example, a child who is bright and inquisitive and accustomed to an educational environment that encourages exploration and experimentation will be unhappy with, and eventually resistant toward, a rigid and formalized class on Sunday morning. In reverse, a child who is accustomed to a strict and disciplined atmosphere during the week and who prefers this type structure, may feel uneasy in, or overwhelmed by, a free give-and-take situation in Sunday school. The benefit of Sunday school will depend on the quality of the educational experience and on its suitability for a particular child. In any case, Sunday school is an addition to the worship services of the church and the training at home.

Are you suggesting that we choose a Sunday school separately from our choice of a church?

Of course, you can't choose a Sunday school separately, or totally, on the basis of its own merits.

The Place of Ritual and Doctrine

What's important to remember is that Sunday school is a choice—for us and for our children—and not a God-given requirement. Over the years, we have acquired the idea that Sunday school is the summation of what the church has to offer children, and that consequently, whether we teach them at home or not, whether we take them to church or not, whether the Sunday school offers good instruction or not, our children *ought* to go. It is true that we cannot raise them as Christians unless we raise them in the church, but the church and the Sunday school, even for children, are not to be equated. Sunday school may well augment their Christian training and their church experience, but it is not where the full burden, or even the major burden, of Christian training ought to rest. After all, when our Lord said,"Upon this rock I will build my church," he did not add "and Sunday school."

Sunday school did not originate until the late eighteenth century, when an educated man named Robert Raikes took pity on poor children working in factories in England and sought to teach them to read and write. Using the Scriptures as his textbook, he began holding classes on Sunday afternoon, and out of this endeavor The Ragged School, forerunner of our Sunday school, was founded in Gloucester in 1780.

We need to keep in mind that Sunday school is a means to an end and that, like other educational efforts, its worth can be judged on the basis of how well it achieves that end. In other words, in making decisions about Sunday school for our children, let's not lose sight of its basic purpose, which properly is to help us raise them "in the nurture and admonition of the Lord."

Train Up Your Child

What should we do if we like everything about our church except the Sunday school?

If we don't feel that the Sunday school measures up to our criteria, for ourselves or for our children, we have little choice but either to become involved and work toward a better program, or not to participate. Which of these options we ought to choose depends on some givens, such as our personal preferences and abilities, and on other easier-to-change factors, such as our schedule and the commitment of our time, energy, and attention elsewhere.

What benefits does becoming involved in Sunday school offer?

It gives us one more opportunity to share in a learning experience with our children; it gives us the opportunity, in conjunction with our children, to share in a Christian learning experience with other families and thus strengthens our commitment to the church. No doubt we will reap what we sow and benefit in proportion to how much we contribute.

What can we do if the Sunday school is offering a good experience to everyone in the family, except one child?

If everyone else in the family is participating, arranging another option for one child may not be convenient. Changing the situation in that one class during the child's time there also may not be an option. Offering the child support by empathizing with his or her reaction to the class may be the best option available, but it is not a solution. Difficult situations like these, however, teach children how to cope with problems and can serve to draw us closer

The Place of Ritual and Doctrine

together, if we recognize their difficulty and sympathize with them.

*And so, in summary, what are we saying about Christian **training** of our children?*

We are saying that, as Christian parents, Christian training is always our highest priority. It is a living-out of the Christian experience with our children, as we fellow travelers find our way together. The years of experience, the daily illustration of Christian principles, the repetition and repetition and repetition, result in our having offered ourselves as examples—not as finished products, but as children of God, ever in process.

*And what are we saying about Christian **teaching**?*

We are saying that *teaching* about the Christ and his church is not enough by itself and that it must be done in conjunction with Christian *training*. Together, training and teaching can enable us to fulfill our charge as Christian parents, to raise our children in the nurture and admonition of the Lord, that they may grow in wisdom and stature and favor with God and man.

CHAPTER NINE

Releasing Our Children

Our children are gifts to us; we have them on loan during their growing years. They are not possessions to keep and hold. From the day they are born, we must begin to prepare them, and ourselves, for letting go. Just as growing up is the goal of childhood, children's independence is the goal of good parenting.

How do we prepare to let them go?

We practice—one step at a time. First we let them stay with baby-sitters, then we let them go next door, then to nursery school and kindergarten and school. We let them ride tricycles to the end of the block and then bicycles to the store. We let them go on trips to visit grandparents and then to camp and, eventually, to Europe. We sit with them in the sandbox, then we hide behind the curtains and watch them play with the neighbor children, and then we tell them to be home by suppertime. Hand in hand, we take them to school, then we put them on the school bus, and then we send them off to college. We are always there if they need us, but if all goes well and according to schedule, they will need us less and less.

Releasing Our Children

How do we know when they are ready to leave home for good?

By trial and error. We—and they—test what they can handle, a little bit at a time, as they are growing up, and eventually, with lots of support and loving encouragement from us, they will want to try their independence.

But what if we don't think they are ready?

Seek advice. Sometimes we not only can't see ourselves as others see us but we can't see our children objectively, either. Because we don't want to lose them or see them make mistakes, we may not be willing to give them the freedom they need. An outside opinion might be helpful.

If our children are of legal age and want to leave before they are truly capable of handling independence, we may have to let them go anyway—leaving the door open for them to come back.

If they leave against our advice, should we let them come back?

We have a biblical example in the parable of the prodigal son, showing us how to welcome our children home.

What constitutes release?

Physical care. There comes a time when we have to let them go physically. This means we have to trust them to take care of themselves, and we no longer have the right, much less any business, to tell them when to get haircuts, when to change their underwear, when to go to bed, when to get up, or what to eat. After so many years with us, they will know when we are pleased and when we are not, but we no longer can try to bring influence to bear. If we have not taught them good habits of health, hygiene, and cleanliness by this time, it is too late.

Social contacts. When they are young we not only have the right, but the obligation, to influence and control their choice of friends, but when they are grown, that right is no longer ours. Then we must accept their choice of friends, business associates, and mates with good grace.

Emotional well-being. Now we must release them to experience pain, even if we believe it to be of their own making; failure, even when we can see how it might be avoided; joy, even in things we do not understand; and triumph, even in areas we do not value. Parents who have made their children the center of their universe falter here. For them, their children's emotional focus on anything other than them, the parents, is unbearable, and efforts to hold onto them lead to unhappiness and frustration for both.

Intellectual development. What they learn or fail to learn is no longer our responsibility. Many parents view their offspring as "projects" they set out to perfect, first by zeroing in on their talents and abilities and then by promotion. They become managers, public relations agents, and judges. The gifts the children possess no longer belong to them but to their parents, who may never stop supervising the music lessons, the scholarship applications, and the career planning. Sooner or later children need to win or lose alone, and we need to permit them to take the risk of failure. Parents who realize early where the responsibility for the homework assignment, the scout badge project, or the piano practice belongs,

Releasing Our Children

will be able to release their children intellectually.

Financial support. Independence, in part, means to be self-supporting. As long as our children receive financial support from us, they are accountable to us, to some extent. No one should be expected to send allowance, supplement income, or pay tuition without being consulted as to the plans and decisions involved. As difficult as we may find it to deny our children what they want, we need to say no, rather than grant financial support when we, in good conscience, cannot grant moral support. Resentment is inevitable if we permit ourselves to be persuaded to provide funds for something we oppose, regardless of the nature of our objections.

Spiritual fulfillment. Spiritually, we must reach a time when we can say to our children and, we hope and pray, they to us, "We are brothers and sisters in the Lord. We all make mistakes; we all ask and receive forgiveness. We accept one another even as God accepts us." Then we can permit them to make their own decisions about Christ as Lord and Savior, interpret for themselves the message of the Good News, define their own role in the work of the church, and live out their own identity as Christian people. Their decisions, interpretations, definitions, and identity may not resemble ours, but they are no longer subject to our supervision, and their values are not determined by our opinion.

Now we move into a new phase of parenting. We guide by example rather than by precept; we speak to our children's Maker, rather than to them, about their behavior; we expect good things of them, rather than require that they measure up to our expectations. We can take our cue from Mary, the mother of

Jesus. After he reached manhood and began his public ministry, she attended a wedding feast with him. Upon realizing that their host was in an embarrassing predicament, she found her son and told him the wine was running out, obviously in the expectation that he would solve the problem. He answered her, "It isn't yet my time" (John 2:4). She didn't argue but evidently continued to expect good things of him, because she instructed the servants to do as he said. And he, as we know, measured up to her expectations.

But what if our children don't measure up to our expectations?

We have to let them go anyway—in hope and fear, and still expecting good things.

Even if we have failed as parents?

We all fail as parents. And even if we did not, we would have no guarantee that our children would turn out to be the kind of people we want them to be. Regardless of our best efforts, they are going to turn out to be themselves. Most of us see our children go out into the world feeling we learned too much too late. We want to call them back and say, "Wait. Give us one more chance to fix this" or "Let's take another try at straightening that out." But now it is, indeed, too late, and efforts on our part to "work on them" can only jeopardize a new relationship with them as adults. A residue of generalized guilt and regret can burden us, and them, until it destroys any hope of a future loving relationship. We need always to hold ourselves accountable for our mistakes, but our efforts should be directed toward the present, and this means letting go of the past. Thomas Merton, the

Catholic monk and writer, spoke of letting go in a way that applies here.

> I have tried to learn in my writing a monastic lesson I could probably not have learned otherwise: to let go of my idea of myself, to take myself with more than one grain of salt. . . . In religious terms, this is simply a matter of accepting life, and everything in life, as a gift and clinging to none of it, as far as you are able. You give some of it to others without bothering too much about how they like it, either, or how they accept it. And if they don't need it, why should they accept it? That is their business.

Where do we find the strength to let our children go?

Consider the alternatives. No good can come of continuing to hold onto them or of letting them continue to hold onto us. When the time comes, it is right and the natural order that they should be on their own. As Paul said, "When I was a child, I spake as a child, I understood as a child, I thought as a child: but when I became a man, I put away childish things"(I Cor. 13:11 KJV). With a giant leap of faith, we brought them into this world; with another giant leap of faith, we release them into it. Neither time do we know what to expect; both times we can only hope for the best.

What parting gifts can we give our children?

They leave home with a legacy: a name and a tradition that we have provided. The legacy may also include property and position, money and opportunity. But what greater gifts can we give our children than the knowledge that one Name is above all names, that a tradition of service to God is to be sought above all others, and that our only enduring treasure lies in the kingdom of heaven?

Train Up Your Child

Then at last we send them into the world with our love and support, looking forward to every possible occasion for showing affection, interest, encouragement, pride, and confidence, that they may always know we wish them Godspeed and rejoice in them and their lives.

ANNOTATED BIBLIOGRAPHY

Andrews, Sheryl J. *Our Children, Our Friends.* Nashville: Thomas Nelson, 1977. Spiritual training of children in a community of Christians.

Baumrind, Diana. "The Development of Instrumental Competence Through Socialization." *Minnesota Symposia on Child Psychology* 7:3-36. Minneapolis: University of Minnesota Press, 1973. Permissive, authoritarian, and authoritative parenting models and the results.

Berends, Polly Berrien. *Whole Child—Whole Parent.* New York: Harper's Magazine Press, 1975. Spiritual and practical guide to the first four years with quotations from the Bible, Buddhism, and Taoism. Approximately 500 books are annotated.

Brazelton, T. Berry. *Infants and Mothers: Differences in Development.* New York: Dell Books, 1969. Discusses developmental patterns of average, active, and quiet infants by a pediatrician who sees a wide range of "normal" behaviors and responses.

Briggs, Dorothy C. *Your Child's Self-Esteem: The Key to His Life.* Garden City, N.Y.: Doubleday & Co., 1974. The focus of this book is on helping children develop a positive self-concept.

Campbell, D. Ross. *How to Really Love Your Child.* Wheaton, Ill.: Victor Books, 1977. A Christian psychiatrist discusses ways parents can love their children that the children can believe and accept.

Capon, Robert Farrar. *The Supper of the Lamb.* New York: Pocket Books, 1970. A book of parents' commitment to each other and to their children from a patriarchal point of view.

Chess, Stella, and Alexander, Thomas. *Temperament and Behavior Disorder in Children.* New York: New York University Press, 1968. Children are influenced not only by environment but by their own personal traits, which may explain why some children are more prone to difficulties and more challenging to parents.

De Palma, David J., and Foley, Jeannie M., eds. *Moral Development: Current Theory and Research.* Hillsdale, N.J.: Lawrence Erlbaum Associates, 1975.

Dobson, James. *The Strong-willed Child: Birth Through Adolescence.* Wheaton, Ill.: Tyndale House, 1978. Author of *Hide and Seek* (dealing with self-esteem in children) and *Dare to Discipline,* writes about handling very assertive children.

Dodson, Fitzhugh. *How to Parent.* Signet; New York: New American Library, 1970. A practical guide to dealing with key problems during the first five years.

Doris, Dennis A. "Teaching Moral Education: Principles of Instruction." *Peabody Journal of Education,* October 1978, pp. 33-44. Clarification of the meaning of "moral education" and how it can be taught.

Erikson, Erik. *Childhood and Society.* 2d ed. New York: W. W. Norton & Co., 1963. Classic statement of Erikson's eight stages of man's development.

Bibliography

Evans, Colleen Townsend. *Teaching Your Child to Pray: A Book You and Your Child Can Read Together*. Garden City, N.Y.: Doubleday & Co., 1978. Photographs and text, for adult and child to share.

Fowler, James, and Keen, Sam. *Life Maps: Conversations on the Journey of Faith*. Edited by Jerome Berryman. Waco, Tex.: Word Books, 1978. Berryman introduces Fowler's discussion of stages of faith development and Keen's discussion of trust. The final section is a dialogue between Fowler and Keen.

Fraiberg, Selma H. *The Magic Years: Understanding and Handling the Problems of Early Childhood*. New York: Charles Scribner's Sons, 1959. Readable discussion of problems children face from birth to five years and how parents can help. Chapter 8 includes an excellent discussion of discipline, punishment, and spanking.

Gesell, Arnold, & Ilg, Frances. *Infant and Child in the Culture of Today*. New York: Harper & Brothers, 1943. Classic statement of physical and social stages of "normal" growth.

Ginott, Haim. *Between Parent and Child*. New York: The Macmillan Co., 1965. Helps parents understand children's feelings and deal with their behavior.

Goldman, Ronald. *Readiness for Religion: A Basis for Developmental Religious Education*. New York: The Seabury Press, 1965. Part I deals with the psychological basis for religious development and explains how religious education should be affected by current educational theory and practice. Part II examines the content and methods of teaching consistent with the healthy development of children and adolescents.

Goldman, Ronald. *Religious Thinking from Childhood to Adolescence*. New York: The Seabury Press, 1964. How children perceive God and spiritual concepts.

Gordon, Thomas. *Parent Effectiveness Training.* New York: Peter H. Wyden, 1970. PET's approach to better parent/child relationships.

Howard, Jane. *Families.* New York: Avon Books, 1978. A study of family styles in America.

Jersild, Arthur T.; Telford, Charles W.; and Sawrey, James M. *Child Psychology.* 7th ed. Englewood Cliffs, N.J.: Prentice-Hall, 1976. Chapter 23 is on moral development, its sources and relation to conscience.

Levine, Milton, and Seligmann, Jean. *The Parents' Encyclopedia of Infancy, Childhood, & Adolescence.* rev. ed. Perennial Library; New York: Harper & Row, 1978. A book with 775 pages of items related to children's health and well-being. Short, precise paragraphs of information on a variety of topics, in alphabetical order.

Lockwood, Alan L. "The Effects of Values Clarification and Moral Development Curricula on School-Age Subjects: A Critical Review of Recent Research." *Review of Educational Research.* Summer 1978, pp. 325-64. A description and review of research related to values clarification originally espoused by Raths, Harmin, and Simon (1966) and moral development derived from work of Kohlberg.

MacDonald, Gordon. *The Effective Father.* Wheaton Ill.: Tyndale House, 1977.

Maddux, Rachel. *The Orchard Children.* New York: Avon Books, 1977. The story of two children who were neglected, taken into a foster home, denied adoption. What rights do children have? How can decisions be made, based on children's needs rather than on adults' desires?

Maier, Henry. *Three Theories of Child Development.* rev.

ed. New York: Harper & Row, 1969. Theories of Erikson, Piaget, and Sears are discussed.

Maslow, Abraham H. *Religions, Values, and Peak-Experiences*. New York: Viking Press, 1964. Maslow extends his thinking beyond his hierarchy, toward self-actualization.

Meier, Paul D. *Christian Child-Rearing and Personality Development*. Grand Rapids: Baker Book House, 1977. A Christian psychiatrist thoroughly discusses all aspects of growth—physical, mental, emotional, spiritual, and sexual.

Murray, Andrew. *How to Raise Your Children for Christ*. Minneapolis: Bethany Fellowship, 1975. Excellent source for parents interested in training children for a lifetime of service.

Narramore, Bruce. *Help! I'm a Parent*. Grand Rapids: Zondervan Publishing House, 1972. Combines practical insights of modern psychology with biblical teachings on child-raising.

Piaget, Jean. *The Moral Judgment of the Child*. New York: The Free Press, 1965. Classic discussion of research on moral development of children.

Stewart, Suzanne. *Parent Alone*. Waco. Tex.: Word Books, 1978. The problems of a single parent learning to lean on God in coping with emotional, financial, and other assorted problems with children.

Strauss, Richard L. *Confident Children and How They Grow*. Wheaton, Ill.: Tyndale House, 1975. God as the model for effective parenthood.

Swarthout, Glendon. *Bless the Beasts and Children*. New York: Pocket Books, 1970. The story of a group of misfit teenagers supporting one another, helping one another grow.

Swindoll, Charles R. *You and Your Child*. Nashville:

Thomas Nelson, 1977. The parent/child relationship and how it relates to spiritual training.

Tillich, Paul. *The Eternal Now.* New York: Charles Scribner's Sons, 1963.

Ton, Mary Ellen. *For the Love of My Daughter.* Elgin, Ill.: David C. Cook, 1978. A hard-to-manage child grows into a rebellious, difficult young adult. The change that occurs in both daughter and mother is described.

White, Burton. *The First Three Years of Life.* Englewood Cliffs, N.J.: Prentice-Hall, 1975. A detailed guide for parents to the intellectual and emotional development of children from birth to thirty-six months.

Wilcox, Mary M. *Developmental Journey: A Guide to the Development of Logical and Moral Reasoning and Social Perspective.* Nashville: Abingdon, 1979.

Wright, Logan. *Parent Power: A Guide to Responsible Childrearing.* New York: Psychological Dimensions, 1978. Principles of human behavior are discussed, and their affect on family interaction described. Appendix includes sections on special problems.